Authentic Pursuit

Building a Church from Nothing

Corey Trimble and Josh
Brooker

Authentic Pursuit: Building a Church from Nothing

Copyright © 2015 by The Experience Christian Community

The Experience Christian Community

521 Old Salem Rd. Suite B

Murfreesboro, TN 37130

Ordering Information:

Quantity sales. Special discounts are available on quantity purchases by corporations, associations, and others. For details, contact the publisher at the address above.

Printed in the United States of America

2015

Authentic Pursuit: Building a Church from Nothing

Authentic Pursuit: Building a Church from Nothing

Authentic Pursuit: Building a Church from Nothing

CONTENTS

Authentic Pursuit: Building a Church from Nothing

Preface

When God called me and my wife to start a church, it seemed to come at a very inconvenient time in our lives. We were working at an affluent denominational church in a great city with a large budget and a great salary package. I was speaking at churches all around the country and making quite a name for myself in student ministry. We had just purchased a home, starting to plan for children, and had strong support from the people in our church. In fact, I was to be to successor to my pastor and was on track to inherit the church that employed me. All of this would change drastically as you will see in the first chapter of this book.

When I finally accepted the call to start a church, I started looking for proper resources to get me on the path of planting a healthy church in our city. I bought almost every book I could find on the subject and read them all at least once, some two and three times over trying to make sure I knew all of the most effective plans to implement and get our church running smoothly and efficiently.

There was a huge problem though. Most if not all of the books I read only worked if certain elements already existed; you had a tithe-paying team already committed, you had denominational support, you could travel and gain financial backers from other churches, or you were wealthy. I had none of these things going for me! So, I was left with very little useful information from these resources. Don't get me wrong, some information was extremely useful, but overall, if one wanted to start a church from nothing, there were no real resources to help plant the church. That is the reason I decided to write this book; to help people like me plant a healthy church with absolutely no outside help other than God.

For those of you reading this right now, believe me, it can be done! If God has called you to do this and if you are doing it for the right reasons, it absolutely can be done. Also, keep in mind that no one formula is the "magic" ingredient to build a successful church. But these tools, plus a total dependence on God, can get you started on building a great, healthy, and growing church. Also remember that God gives each person a vision that is unique to them. God does not want cookie-cutter counterfeit church plants. He wants you to use your talent and intellect to create Christ-followers in your city. Do not be afraid to be unorthodox and different. As long as you are in the Word of God and seeking His will, methodology can be as unique as your mind will let it be.

When Paul was in the beginning stages of his work for Christ, a wise man on the Sanhedrin council stated that if the work Paul is doing is of himself and for his own gain, it will fail. But, this wise man then stated that if it is of God and done for His Kingdom, no man can stop him.

I wish you the best, and may God bless your work!

Pastor Corey Trimble

Authentic Pursuit: Building a Church from Nothing

CHAPTER 1

I NEEDED CONVINCING

"Indeed, we have all received grace after grace from His fullness," (John 1:16)

Authentic Pursuit: Building a Church from Nothing

I needed more convincing than most, I guess.

I wish I could say that I came into Christianity easily. However, like many people, it took a little convincing via some troublesome times for me to become a follower of Christ.

I wasn't really raised in a Christian home. My parents were church-goers until I was eleven years old, but their marriage was pretty rocky and we weren't extremely committed. My folks had decided to get a divorce when I was around twelve, and though my memory is absolutely terrible most of the time, I can recall almost every step I took the night my parents sat me down in our living room and told me that they were going to "spend some time apart." My mother was going to live in St. Louis and my father in Nashville. Needless to say, divorce is always difficult, and with my parents' divorce came the typical issues. My mother almost drowned in regret and my father was left to deal with a soon-to-be teenage boy that for all intents and purposes his ex-wife had raised up until this point. I remember my father attended church avidly for a short period of time, but pretty quickly after the divorce, church and any talk of Jesus was completely absent from my life.

I started to rebel greatly in my teenage years. I started huffing paint and smoking cigarettes with other boys in the neighborhood at age 12, smoked weed for the first time at age 13, and lost my virginity at 14. These things obviously put a wedge in my relationship with my dad. As I got a little older, I got my motorcycle license and started getting into more trouble. I used my new method of transportation to go to parties where I eventually got wrapped up in speed, cocaine, and pills. My Father wasn't a bad man, but he didn't know how to handle me very well. So, when I was 17 years old I packed my bag (literally) and moved out and into my mother's house which was now in Lebanon, TN just 20 minutes or so from my dad.

I went to college at 18 and failed miserably my first year. I cared more about playing music, smoking cigarettes, and watching Scooby Doo at 2a.m. than going to class. I started to tour a lot with a band called High-strung that had a pretty big following around the Southeast playing bass then eventually guitar. With touring and putting out records on various labels came the lifestyle often associated with music-- more parties and acting like an idiot. During this time I also got into stealing electronics from convention centers and selling them on a new ecommerce site called eBay in order to make money to fund trips and our ridiculous drinking binges. Looking back, it must have been God's grace that I never got into really serious trouble with the law, though I did get arrested once.

In my junior year of college all of this wild living came to a head. The girl I had dated for 5 years (and I am married to now) was starting to get fed up with me and my lifestyle, and we eventually broke up for 6 months. I was drinking often and putting music and my ego way ahead of her. Our relationship was quickly falling apart and at the same time the band I was playing in was breaking up. Oddly enough, my health was also starting to worsen as well.

While working at a local record store in town, I passed out for no reason, but I brushed this off thinking that maybe the past drinking and drug use had caught up with me, but after it happened again over lunch with Alicia, I decided to contact a doctor. The first neurologist I saw thought I was stressed from college and my relationship so, again, I brushed it off. The problems started to grow worse, and the motor skills in my hands and legs started to weaken. At 22 years old I could no longer play the guitar or go to work, and eventually I was confined to a wheelchair for several weeks. The second or third neurologist I saw thought it was the beginning stages of Multiple Sclerosis and starting taking measures to treat that. He did the best he could, but little was working as far as medicine. Looking back, I see what God was starting to do to get my attention.

I was stuck. Once upon a time I was traveling, playing music, had a great girlfriend, and was making money hand over fist. Now I was broke, stuck at home, and utterly alone unable to even pick up my guitar to play it because I was physically unstable.

There were some bright spots in this dark time of my life. My father, who I had not talked to in almost five years, was back in my life. He was the bigger man because he put all of our history behind us and started spending time with me. I remember one time while I was really sick that he took me to a car show. He pushed me around in my wheelchair as we looked at vintage cars, and this eventually became a great common ground for us to converse about. God bless old cars. I also saw my mother and father talk for the first time in years. They sat in a waiting room at one of the hospitals where I was doing treatment and getting some tests done and talked with my wife, Alicia. There is a somewhat humorous story about me throwing up and saying multiple expletives in front of all three of them in the foyer after I had blood drawn, but maybe that will be in another book. But for the first time in a long time, I saw some hope. Even though I couldn't identify it yet, God was working in my life.

As I stated earlier, I said that my family went to church when I was a kid. Well, there was a pastor in our city that knew some members of my family in St. Louis and throughout my years in college, he would come by the record store to chat with me about jazz, movies, or whatever.

When all of these events mentioned in the last paragraph happened, Pastor Phil was the only person I could think of to talk with. I literally stumbled into his office half drunk and deprived of sleep one weekday shortly after Alicia had left me and I fell into one of his chairs in his office. At this point, I was at the lowest part of my entire life. I had tried to take my life before, once with pills and once with a gun in my mouth. This time, I had tried to drink myself to death. I had purchased hundreds of dollars of vodka from a local liquor store and locked myself in my room, hoping to just fall asleep and never wake up. But, for some reason, I left my house to go visit a small church down the road.

Phil looked at me with much wisdom and asked if I was ready for a change. I remember telling him that I was tired. I was. I needed to change my life or I think I would have ended it that week. Sometime in that conversation in his office that day at the church I had the most dramatic conversion ever. I lay on the ground as people, that to this day I am not sure who they were, prayed for me. I remember crying and "snotting" all over everyone I could get my hands on and telling God how sorry I was about a billion times. I was filled with His Spirit that Wednesday in August and I was never to be the same again. Phil and I talked for a while before I let out a huge yawn. I recall him almost jumping out of his seat saying, "Look! God is already starting to give you rest!" It was a brilliant observation. He was right, God was about to give me a peace and rest like I had never known.

The following Sunday morning I jumped headfirst into attending and then serving at that church. From here on, my life would never be the same.

I needed more convincing than most, but eventually I believed.

My wife, who at this time was just my girlfriend (well actually we were broken up, so…nothing I guess), was also not a Christian, and had a hard time believing that my conversion experience had any validity to it at all. For the following 6 months after I became a Christian I tried so hard to reconnect with the woman I had loved, then shoved away through my reckless lifestyle. I would invite her to church, I bought her a bible with her name on it, and would constantly try to show her this thing I had found, but to no avail. Eventually I got her to come to a service in January of 2003. Of course it was one of those "freaky" services that sometimes happen at Pentecostal churches where people are on the floor moaning and people are praying in tongues into the microphone. I remember "crazy tambourine lady" banging away and "run around the church man" speedily passing us in the sanctuary. Needless to say she got a little freaked out.

After spouting a couple of select expletives, she convinced me to take her home. But, on the way home something interesting happened. Alicia literally began to slump down in my car into the floorboard and scream. Yes, this was a demonic battle going on in my car! Without saying anything, I turned around and went back to the church and pulled up to the front. I took Alicia out and carried her into the sanctuary kicking and screaming.

I laid her down on a pew and got my pastor's attention. Phil came back and prayed with Alicia as several other people joined in via laying on of hands. I remember that night very well. Alicia relented to a God that she wasn't even sure existed an hour before service and was filled with His Spirit and baptized as a Christian. I guess we both needed more convincing than most.

The point of my testimony is not to brag on my past mistakes or even to show the glaring contrast of my previous life compared to my current walk with God. The point is this: anyone is capable of leading for the cause of Christ. Pedigree is not required, affluence is not mandatory, and mistakes simply make one wiser and more qualified to minister to and sympathize with the very people you may lead. If I can be called to minister to people, anyone can!

From floor-mopper to student pastor

After becoming a Christian in 2002, I quickly dove into any kind of work I could at our local church. I remember going up to my former pastor and asking what I could do, knowing I was not qualified in any way to teach or lead, but also knowing that I needed to have a purpose in order to survive as a Christian. Unbelievable as it may seem (me being this guy covered in tattoos and piercings) he gave me a key to the whole facility because I became the guy that arrived too early, and stayed too late. I loved being in the church. I asked again, "What can I do?" and Pastor said something to the effect of, "Well, the floors need cleaning."

That is how true ministry starts. Often at conferences and seminars people will ask how I got started. I simply say I picked up a mop and I mopped the church floors. No one wants to hear that kind of answer. They want to be given a mike and 300 people to yell at and be instantly propelled to some rock star status, but no one wants to clean the floors for Jesus. My favorite image of God is the one from Bruce Almighty. Bruce sees God for the first time, and what is God doing? He is upstairs cleaning the floor with a mop.

Authentic Pursuit: Building a Church from Nothing
That is so God, up there cleaning up our mess, doing the job no one wants to do.

So, for at least a year or so I did this kind of work around our church. I also started a Bible study at a local coffee shop where I worked. This was a great place! It was called the Red Rose, and it was the cultural hot spot of our college town and a great place to witness to the kind of people that I was once a part of and could identify with. The Red Rose was kind of the epicenter of culture in our small city. We had bands play on the weekends, droves of gay pagan nudists from Short Mountain hung out there all the time (clothed), we sold records and craft beer, and throughout the week they did body suspensions in the back (people hanging by hooks). Yep, you heard that right. Sounds repulsive, but I saw it as a great place to do a Bible study. Though I didn't know much about the Word, the studies went great. We had between 25 and 30 people coming to our study, so we started to break it up between two other coffee shops as well. It was so apostolic, and to this day it is one of the coolest times of my life.

The Red Rose closed down not too long after the Bible studies got going, but I still keep in touch with many of the people from these Bible studies. The buzz from these studies got me enough attention from the church to offer me a Sunday School teacher position with teenagers. I like that. "Hey get the guy who teaches gay nudists to teach our kids the Bible!" The youth group was not that big when I started working in the Sunday School department, maybe 30 kids or so, but I was really

9

excited about the chance to teach in a more structured setting. I did this for a year or so until a position opened up for the Student Pastor position.

I knew instantly that I was the man for the vacant Student Pastor position. Though I was still considered a new convert, just a year and half into my faith, I was sure I was ready to take this task on.

Then a weird thing happened. I prayed and fasted about the Student Pastor spot for some time and got confirmation from God that I would get it. I got this confirmation the day before the job was offered to the Pastor's son, who I felt was not ready at all to take on such a responsibility. This devastated and confused me greatly. I was so sure that God had confirmed in me that this was my place and time, but this transaction was almost the opposite of what God had shown me. I had to sit back and take a secondary position to a younger and, I felt like, entitled pastor's kid who had no real appreciation for this ministry (heck he was barely out of the youth group at all). For almost a full year I watched my pastor's son and his staff, which I was reluctantly a part of, do little with this youth group. It was unorganized, shallow, and a lot of times grossly inappropriate, but in this time of patiently playing second fiddle, God taught me so many lessons about His timing and my long-suffering. Though it was very difficult, I learned how to follow church hierarchy and respect a pastor's decisions though I strongly disagreed. It was definitely a learning time for me.

Authentic Pursuit: Building a Church from Nothing

The pastor's son's time ran out as Student Pastor. Though he had the pedigree and the support of the board, the church as a whole saw no progress in our church for the junior high and high school kids. So, after a year he was removed from his position, and my wife and I were asked out to dinner with our pastor. Our pastor offered me a "job" as Student Pastor with no pay, perks, or benefits, but I didn't care. I knew this was God fulfilling a promise made to me over a year ago. I took it without any hesitation. Looking back, my pastor's son was not a bad guy, but was too young and put into a place prematurely. It wasn't his fault, and I learned so much about timing.

I remember my first service as youth pastor. In the youth room was a big Styrofoam "Y" right in the middle of the stage that looked like it was made of metal. This thing was not only atrocious, but was a huge symbol of the old regime before me. The "Y" stood for, you guessed it, youth. After teaching my first lesson about the vision and direction of this floundering ministry, we had a party after the service and the kids went buck wild. They were acting ridiculous and being very disrespectful to my wife and me. So, by the next service I had totally destroyed that hideous "Y" that stood in the youth room and painted the room a completely different color. Needless to say this upset everyone! But, a point was being made-- the old ways are done, there's a new leader in charge.

The first six months were hard, but over time the group started to buy into the new direction. The group

Authentic Pursuit: Building a Church from Nothing

was about 25 kids when we took it over, but after one year we had about 65 teens showing up. The most miraculous thing is that we were not doing typical youth things. Instead, we dove heavily into the Bible. We covered all of Matthew and Acts in six months and instead of just fun events all the time, we did long stints of prayer and fasting. Believe it or not, teens want large doses of God, not just Xbox and junk food at church!

At this point in my life, I was passionate without much restraint or wisdom. I saw many mistakes, and made many of my own, but I think I learned so much that first year of doing structured ministry and seeing the workings of a church. Things would get better, but some things would get much harder.

CHAPTER 2

BUT I WAS COMFORTABLE...

"But He told him, "Let the dead bury their own dead, but you go and spread the news of the kingdom of God." (Luke 9:60)

Authentic Pursuit: Building a Church from Nothing

I never thought I would be someone who would start a church. Nothing could be farther from my thinking. For one thing, there seemed to be plenty of churches in the cities and communities around me. Before I met the Lord, I was pretty sure my life plan involved me being a rock star, and playing punk rock in front of crowds of adoring fans. God, however, had very different plans for my life.

After I'd gotten saved and started doing ministry in my church and denomination, I began to notice some things about church culture in general that didn't sit well with me.

The first was that it seemed we put an inordinate amount of time, money, energy and resources into ourselves at the expense of the community around us. The events we organized, the trips we took, and the conferences we held- they were all planned by us and for people exactly like us, and nobody seemed especially bothered by that. There were homeless people in our city, families struggling just to make ends-meet in the neighborhoods around us, and yet we seemed to make meeting our own needs for socialization, fellowship, and encouragement as a church more of a priority than meeting the needs of the community around us. Money was raised and spent on building projects and elaborate events, but there weren't a lot of resources given to community organizations that were meeting the physical needs of the poor. Over time this started to really bother me.

Another thing that didn't sit well with me was the lack of acceptance we showed towards people who didn't look or act like us. The first time my wife (who was my girlfriend at the time) came to church as an agnostic (I say atheist) who did some modeling on the side and spent time in dance clubs in downtown Nashville, she was wearing skintight, electric red pants (I kid you not!). It was a big deal that she had even agreed to come to church in the first place, so I was nervous when we pulled into the parking lot and walked in together through the front door. When the woman stationed near the front of the sanctuary entrance saw the two of us, she made a snide remark about how Alicia was dressed inappropriately for church. It was frustrating and hurtful to me how someone who had no idea how long I had prayed and how many times I had begged my girlfriend to come to church could negatively affect her experience before she even walked through the door. *Even though Jesus spent a lot of his time around prostitutes, tax collectors, sinners, thugs and people we wouldn't want our kids hanging out with, we had a bad habit of accepting people conditionally.* The truth is, irreligious people felt comfortable around Jesus. He radically accepted people from all walks of life and changed them from the inside out with love. But too many times as a church if outsiders didn't look like us, talk like us or act like us, we tended to withhold our acceptance of them until they got their act together. So naturally, new people who were different from us tended to not stick around, which really hindered us from being able to lead them to the Lord and see God do something miraculous in their lives. There was a definite divide between "insiders" and "outsiders", and it took a long time for someone to become an "insider" and learn the secret church code words and the appropriate dress codes for all of our services.

Meanwhile, the kind of crowd I was used to hanging out with were the kind of people who wouldn't darken the door of a church like the one I worked at. People like the ones I had led in Bible study at the Red Rose- artists, musicians, hipsters, loners, outsiders, and all of the "fringe" people who were never accepted by the rest of the world. They were deep-thinkers that asked hard questions. Where were the churches for those people? Who was going to take the gospel to a community so desperately different from what we were comfortable with inside of our own subculture?

So I decided to start one. I decided to answer the call I felt like God had put on my heart to start a church that took ownership of the community around us and met the needs of the poor. I felt like God wanted this church to be a place where irreligious people would feel welcomed and valued because they've been made in the image of God. *A church where people didn't just hear about the love and grace of God- they experienced the love and grace of God for themselves.*

While I was still working as a student pastor, I took a few days off, went out of town and spent some time with my laptop and the persistent, God-sized ideas that had been churning in my head and heart. I typed out a 13 page model of what I felt like God was calling me to start. The church would be called "The Experience Community"- a Biblically based, brutally honest community open to believers and seekers. We'd be simple- very simple. Every week we'd do verse by verse, chapter by chapter study of the Bible, we'd worship through song, we'd love and serve each other as community, and we'd focus on meeting the needs of the poor and needy within our city. The one word I couldn't stop repeating was *authentic*. Would we have all the answers? No, but we would pursue them with honesty and transparency.

Something that is authentic is genuine, credible, and believable. I was done playing church. I wanted to create something that was real. If people were broken and hurting when they came to church, I wanted them to be comfortable admitting where they were. If we claimed to be a place of love, acceptance, forgiveness and grace, I wanted us to actually be that. I wanted us to be real. Authentic. Genuine. I wanted us to say what we meant and to mean what we said.

When I returned from my trip, I was excited to announce to my pastor my intent to start a church and I gave him my 13-page model. I originally thought that the Experience Community might be a daughter work of my home church, but in that first meeting with my pastor it became apparent to me very quickly that that wasn't going to happen. It's a bit of an understatement to say that I did not get the support or encouragement from my former pastor that I thought I would. The last thing I ever wanted to do was to divide my church or cause a church split. I just wanted to be obedient to what I felt God was calling me to do. But that was difficult for me to communicate because it felt like my dreams were being seen as direct attacks against my home church. They were scared, and oddly enough, I get it.

Even though I was open and transparent about my intentions, there was a fear that I was going to split the church with my little church plant. My wife and I knew the time for me as a student pastor at the church was coming to an end. I no longer felt like I belonged there and it was becoming clear to me that the leadership was suspicious of my intentions. After a lot of prayer and thought, I decided to announce my resignation to my pastor because the last 4 months or so after declaring my intentions of starting a church, it got really uncomfortable. The day I formally resigned, I asked my pastor if I could have a couple of weeks to get everything in order so I could exit in a way that wasn't hurtful or damaging. He wanted me gone by the end of the week. Again, I get it. I was a potential threat and a "danger" to their theology and comfort. I remember that day well. Before I could even tell my wife I had quit, people from 3 other states were calling me asking about me quitting. News, or gossip I should say, travels fast in the church world.

As shocking and hurtful as the response to my resignation was, what happened next I could have never prepared for. On a Sunday night shortly after we left, my former pastor, employer, and spiritual advisor gave a public speech to the congregation condemning us and our actions. The church was told that we had been sent by Satan to divide and destroy the church body, and we were completely "disfellowshipped" (or excommunicated) by the church. Not only that, my wife and I were officially excommunicated and shunned by my entire denomination, other church leadership and most of the friends we had come to know and love over the years. The pain and shock was almost unbearable. In the days after our departure and subsequent blacklisting by the church leadership, I waited for friends and family to call and console us. The calls never came. In fact, to this day if I see members of that church in a grocery store or at a restaurant, they sometimes walk the opposite direction. There are members of my family that are in that same denomination who to this day have never met my children and refused to speak to us at my grandfather's funeral.

You know, looking back I realize more that I was not a good fit in that church's culture, so God was pushing me out. I also realized it wasn't really my place to change a church that hadn't invited me to do so. Essentially it was a bad fit both ways. It was still a tough pill to swallow though. I was hurt, angry, confused, and scared all at the same time. In a few short years I had encountered God, found a new church family, gotten married, and enjoyed a tremendous amount of success in ministry within this denomination. Then the unthinkable happened right when I started to take the next step of faith. I had lost all my friends and my family and had no real direction. I was depressed and wondered if I'd made the right decision.

If this was God's will for me, why in the world was it so unbelievably painful and difficult? I remember being so depressed and confused that I would lie awake most nights on the couch downstairs in our condo staring at the TV I wasn't really watching. One night as I was dosing off on the couch in the wee hours of the morning, my wife woke me up holding a pregnancy test that read "positive". We were going to have a baby. I had no job, no clear plan of direction, and no friends or family to share this quiet miracle with. Was this really God's plan for me?

At times it was hard to even pray. It was hard to even read the Bible. I wanted to tell God, "Don't you know what I am going through here? I mean, I have done it all right! Right? I gave you my all!" I felt completely inadequate, lost, and helpless. I felt like the religious machine had crippled me and left me for dead. On top of everything I just felt lonely. But in the midst of all of the pain, anger, and confusion, I still had a quiet and steady certainty in my calling from the Lord to start a church. At times it seemed like an improbable fantasy, but I knew what God wanted me to do. *Every day I had to return to total and complete dependence on God. Without it, I would self-destruct.*

I happened to resign from my position at the church in the midst of the one of the worst economic recessions our nation has ever faced. Timing has never been my strong suit. I went from enjoying a very comfortable compensation package at my old church to being unemployed for 2 ½ months. I couldn't find work anywhere! Every day I would send out resumes, only to get nothing in return for my efforts. Money was tight, very tight, and the stress was getting to me. One day that summer we started the day with less than $10 to our name. With the last bit of cash we had in our house, $3 in nickels, I got some gas to drive to Starbucks to meet two friends.

I met with two of the guys that were helping start the church for a brain storming session on the two websites that we would have for the church. After a long 3 hour meeting, a friend of mine, that had also been through a tough church separation, wanted to speak to me outside. I went outside Starbucks and sat next to him. He then proceeded to give me $100 and told me to take out my wife to get our minds off all of the stress we had been dealing with. In the midst of our storm, God was still faithful. I'm still really good friends with Ken, and he comes to the church today.

I finally got a part time job cleaning toilets in a factory on the night shift, and I also found work at a community and business college teaching intro level English classes for the fall semester. That summer I had started mapping out and planning with my very small team what the first step looked like to begin launching a church. But there was a problem. All of the books I picked up talked about things I had no idea about and no access to. They talked about going to your church or denomination or seeking out donors. I had none of these. The church I left did not provide any support either spiritually, emotionally, and certainly not financially. I didn't have the backing of a church; I had no kind of financial help at all. All I had was a small group of dedicated people and a dream. I remember when I started the church, the only person that completely caught onto the vision was a guy named Stephen Belk. Though Stephen works in an important corporate job, he holds a certain mystique at our church and is involved in many of the things we do. Looking back, if it wasn't for him believing in me, I'm not sure I would have had the courage to do all I have.

The one idea that was doable in my situation was the idea of holding "preview services". The basic idea behind this strategy is to start out holding monthly preview services as a way to gather more people into the launch team so that you can ideally double your team. This phase allows you to continue to focus on gathering and ministering to people, communicating the vision of the church, and raising enough financial support to be able to launch the church plant effectively. Far too often, new church plants are so consumed with having to plan for worship each week and gather enough volunteers to actually make church happen that they don't have time to focus on things like that. Preview services should be heavily promoted via social media, fliers, print ads, word of mouth and basically any medium available to let as many people in the community know that something new is starting up. We only promoted in areas and places that Christians typically don't hangout. We put stuff in bars, tattoo parlors, coffee shops, and in publications that mostly artsy people would read. Our goal wasn't to shuffle people who already believe or to "sheep steal," but to make new disciples of Christ.

With some money that God provided through our very small team, we were able to secure a spot on Sunday nights in an auditorium in the Murfreesboro Center for the Arts for our four monthly preview services. My wife and I would tithe to a bank account set up under the churches name and we got one other couple to do the same. A local newspaper ran an article on me and the church, and we also launched a website and a "campaign" (by campaign, I mean me on MySpace) on social media to help us get the word out about the services. Things were moving in the right direction, but it was a bit surreal and hard to believe that we were actually going to be starting a church.

The closer we got to the first monthly service, the more frustrated I became with some of the people helping us. Only one couple put up any money towards the plant besides us, and I had to do all the preparation except for the non-profit application that another couple had volunteered to complete. In spite of the difficulties, the excitement was starting to build. I knew that I needed to become increasingly committed to prayer and fasting, and that God will shine through all of this regardless of my shortcomings and attitude problems.

On the day of our first monthly preview service, I was excited, but I had no idea what to expect. For all I

Authentic Pursuit: Building a Church from Nothing

knew, there could be 20 or 200 people in attendance, and either one would not surprise me very much. I had done everything I could to prepare for the service: I had promoted and advertised as much as humanly possible, I had planned a service flow, begged some friends of a friend to lead worship, invited as many people as I could and written a lesson that I hoped would communicate our vision and touch peoples' hearts. The rest was in God's hands. I met my "staff" at 3pm to go over everything and make sure that we all would get to the venue on time. The center for the arts was performing Fiddler on the Roof and I wanted to make sure that Tevye had not trashed the whole theatre.

Our first service had 41 people in attendance. It went very well, and we received over $400 in offering. Three people showed up that I had never met that had read the article in the paper. The service only lasted 45 minutes, but there were no technical problems, the music was great, and we had a lot of good responses from the visitors. God really provided. I was grateful that so many people came out, and it felt like we were gathering momentum and gearing up for the next four services.

The people that came out to our preview services were exactly the kind of people I hoped our church would attract. The title of the message for the third preview service was "We apologize for our treatment towards homosexuals." I spent some time apologizing for the un-Christlike and hateful way the church had treated homosexuals, but I also opened the Bible and shared truth about homosexuality being a sin. Even

Authentic Pursuit: Building a Church from Nothing

though what I was sharing is not extremely popular in our culture, we had over 50 people in attendance, including a gay friend of mine and a girl that worked at the adult bookstore down the street. God had blessed us with the real outcasts of society. Lots of people with tattoos, piercings and close to no knowledge about Christ were flooding the church, and it was everything that I had prayed for. On top of that, we had $1,427 given in tithes and offerings in one night!

Our last monthly preview service was in January of 2009. For the first time, our little monthly gatherings were starting to feel like actual church services. After the last preview service, we had a bit of a falling out with the Center for the Arts. No one on the board of directors really wanted a church to meet in the facility and the Unitarian Church that also met there didn't like us teaching the Bible exclusively, but no one had the guts to deal with it either. So we decided it was time for us to find our own space. In January, our church signed a lease for a great place in a high-traffic area on the square. God was good, as we landed on awesome underground building for $1550 a month plus utilities.

We purchased 48 chairs for $240 that was donated to us through a silent auction held at Starbucks. The same Starbucks had just recently closed, and I did some dumpster diving afterwards. I managed to score 11 chairs and 7 tables. One night as a friend and I were fishing the chairs and tables in the rain from the dumpster and into a truck, a cop happened to drive by and ask what we were doing. After we told him, he just gave us a weird look and drove off. It's public domain if it's in a dumpster, right?

On the 23rd of January, 2009, the Experience Community moved into our first building. The place was tiny (so small I could palm the ceilings), didn't have heat (we had to set up propane heaters before service and get the place really hot, hoping it would last all night), and had enough space to seat maybe 50 people. We had some things to fix up, but the excitement level was high. We had our own building! It was really happening. People were owning the mission and the vision that I had cast in the preview services and God was sending us a very different and unique group of people for us to minister to.

Around that time I got a job at the Murfreesboro Athletic Club working from 10 PM-6 AM. I knew the church couldn't afford to pay me, and I was fine with that. I was willing to work as hard as I knew how to make the dream that God had given me a reality. We started doing weekly services on February 15th, right around the time our baby girl was born. The first book of the Bible I decided to work through was the book of Matthew. After coming out of a denomination that put so much focus and attention on secondary issues, I wanted our church first and foremost to know who Jesus was. I wanted the newcomers that had never darkened the door of a church to first discover the life-changing truth of Christ.

As a young pastor and Bible teacher, I was still working through some theological and doctrinal issues for myself. The theology of the denomination I came

Authentic Pursuit: Building a Church from Nothing

from tended to lean towards works-based salvation and placed an over-emphasis on speaking in tongues as the sole evidence that someone had the Holy Spirit. Even though now I know the Biblical stance on both, at the time I wasn't quite sure what to make of these issues. Working through the Bible with my young church, verse by verse, chapter by chapter, helped me begin to find clarity in a lot of areas. As a church I think it took us a good two years to shake a lot of the former false teaching and find our doctrinal foundations. It was a slow and messy process, but it's one that any new church plant can't afford to skip.

In that first year we had a baptism service where 9 people were baptized. This was a huge success. We had over 25 people at the baptism class, and the people who chose to get dunked were all newbies to Christianity. One used to work in an adult bookstore, one was involved in witchcraft, and others were former agnostics. God was so good to us.

After we worked through the book of Matthew, we started the book of Acts to see what God's original plan for the church was. I was still working the night shift at the Murfreesboro Athletic Club (the MAC) and watching my infant daughter during the day so my wife could work. The church was going fairly well, but we had had some crazy bumps in the road. First, one of the key members in our church (that helped with the preview services and the launch) left because I told him he could not smoke pot and tell others that God wanted them to do it as well. I found out the mid-week "Bible study" he was hosting at his house involved just as much weed smoking as it did studying the book of Ezekiel.

It seems funny now, but at the time it was pretty serious. Over 30 people left because I stood up to this issue and would not allow such garbage in our church. So, we had a church-split in our first year over pot. What started off as a strong launch, was not stifled. By September, we had about 60 people in our services. We started going to 2 services in order to attract more people and cut out the "double-dippers" that seem to come just for the "hipness" of the church.

Personally, I went through extreme ups and downs. I was exhausted from doing the church, watching my daughter, meeting with people, being called "pastor" and working the night shift at a fitness club. I often had to repent for my bad attitude at work. I sometimes felt like Paul with the reoccurring thorn in his side. For me, that thorn came in many forms: doubt, fear, mental anguish, and lack of trust in God. Few people came into the club in the middle of the night/morning when I worked, but oddly enough, the front desk at the Murfreesboro Athletic Club became the place for me to do most of my studies and occasional mentoring and counseling. Yes, I said counseling. I did premarital counseling at 2 A.M. more than once during my shifts, and several people a week would come up to the club to discuss God and ideas for the church.

That year I discovered that the people that came to our church were there for a variety of reasons, but a lot were there simply because we were new and

Authentic Pursuit: Building a Church from Nothing

different. Some of them were attracted to the novelty of it all- the fact that we were young, we were small, and we met in a tiny basement room off the square. Some of them were truly seeking God but never felt welcomed and comfortable in more traditional churches. Some wore the "I-was-hurt-by-church" label like a badge of honor and showed up with a chip on their shoulder, ready to have all of their demands met or they'd get their feelings hurt and leave. Some of them were simply looking for a "church" or spiritual movement that condoned and endorsed the lifestyle that they already decided to live. When I started taking a solid Biblical stance against things like drug use, getting drunk, sex outside of marriage, and homosexuality, a lot of those people stopped coming. *The one thing I learned is that the group you start with in the first 6 months is not your permanent group of people.* About 9 months in, almost everyone we started with had moved on, minus 10 to 15 people, to other things, places, or beliefs.

Nonetheless, we were doing two services, with the 11am running almost 40 people and the 6pm running about 30 or so. By the fall we had a great new couple coming to church from Los Angeles. They had both been in ministry at another church, one as a teacher and one as a worship leader. The husband started leading worship on Sundays, and his wife was on the fast track to teaching at our church in a small group setting. That fall we started doing communion every week at the end of service. This allowed people to reflect on what

29

had been taught. It also gave me a way to transition the church into a mentality that was more comfortable with prayer and ministry times. People really started looking forward to those times of prayer and communion, and we began to see God move in powerful ways as we made every effort to surrender to the Holy Spirit moving and working in our services. To this day, we still do communion at all our services, which means we prepare thousands of those tiny cups and break many pieces of Matzo bread every weekend. I think those early days were instrumental in weaving that element into our DNA as a church. *We never want to get so large, manicured, or "professional" that God can't have a say in where our service goes. It was easier to uphold this value when we were smaller, but it becomes increasingly difficult the more a church grows.*

We *always* want the Holy Spirit to be the true leader in any and every service or meeting that goes on at our church. If we're there for any other reason than to see God and to experience His power at work amongst us, we're wasting our time. The early believers gathered together each week without a completed version of the Bible, without talented praise bands or catchy worship songs, without lighting systems, soundboards, microphones, or elaborate staging- yet the fruit of those meetings produced Disciples of Christ that would flip the world upside down and change the course of human history. Why? What was the "secret" of their success?

Authentic Pursuit: Building a Church from Nothing

It wasn't a clever sermon series or efficient processes. It wasn't aesthetically pleasing facilities or a polished welcoming committee with gifts for the first time guests, although none of those things are necessarily bad. *It was the power of God. That's something that can't be faked or replicated. That's something you can't buy from a church-planting conference or the Christian bookstore.* In order for this element to be present in your church and in your services, there must be an authentic, heartfelt, genuine desperation for the power of God to show up in everything you do. There must be a willingness to admit your own inadequacy and helplessness apart from the power and presence of God. There's something about servants of God who are keenly aware of their own weakness apart from the Holy Spirit that God loves. The Psalmist writes in Psalms 149: 4, "…the LORD takes pleasure in his people; he adorns the humble with salvation." In other words, God loves to show up and show off when His people humbly seek His presence and power above everything and anything else.

In the years we've been a church, it's not been uncommon for us to see non-believers with no previous knowledge of the Christian faith walk into one of our services out of curiosity and end up encountering the presence of the Holy Spirit in such a tangible way that they're driven to their knees, weeping and crying out to God. I can remember two women, a mother and daughter, who identified themselves as members of the Wiccan faith and had never even been inside a church building until they came to an evening service. Before the teaching even began, the Holy Spirit rocked these two women in such a powerful way during our time of worship that they were shaking, crying, and praying before they even knew how! What was the secret to these women radically encountering the person of Jesus? *It was the power of the Holy Spirit.*

Attempting to move forward with a church plant without seeking the power and anointing of the Holy Spirit is a bit like trying to drive a Stock Car on a mostly empty tank of gas. You might get down the road a little bit, but eventually you'll come to a standstill. We learned early on that apart from a desperate reliance on the Holy Spirit, prayer and a willingness to see God have His way in our services, we weren't going anywhere.

By the end of the year, we were running out of space in our basement room. We actually ran out of space about 2 months before the end of the year, and because of that, we didn't start any of sort of children's, student, or small-group ministries. **We recommend new churches don't even consider doing much more than the Sunday Service their first year.** Eventually, we started looking for a new building for our church. We were considering moving our church a couple of miles away to a much bigger spot, but I wasn't willing to give up a centralized location near the downtown area.

Even though God was working and good things were happening in our church, my wife and I were already on the brink of burn out by the end of our first year. More than anything, we just needed a vacation. We were both working full time and watching our daughter full time as well. We both were planning time to be with people from church, but that was becoming very hard to do. I started getting very frustrated with some of the people coming to the church because of their lack of commitment and abundance of complaining. I guess I had always known that about people, but I had never experienced that level of whining and general lack of spine until I became known as "pastor". My wife was beginning to feel almost exactly like me, but her faith and general niceness are considerably greater than mine.

The potential move was also very scary. Our little place on the square was starting to feel like home, but the new place would be over twice the size and have much more potential to do church the way I felt like God wanted us to do it. The temptation in church planting is to get comfortable and to confuse the goals of the church plant.

We are called to build more Disciples of Christ, not just keep the lights on in the building and the staff's salaries paid. Hear me out- I'm not advocating just "firing from the hip" and moving forward without thinking and praying through big decisions. There is great value in planning, practicing financial wisdom, strategizing, and examining a course of action as a church. Many church planters attempt to justify foolish organizational moves as "leaps of faith", when in reality they're just being poor stewards of the

Authentic Pursuit: Building a Church from Nothing resources God has given them by not thinking and praying through a huge decision thoroughly before acting. There is also equal danger in a church or organization moving too slowly and cautiously instead of exploring their options, praying earnestly, discussing the decision, and just doing something. Far too many churches lose their momentum because they sit back in cowardice and fear, not believing God's promises for their future, instead of boldly stepping out in faith. Big decisions need not be made at a glacial pace if they're made prayerfully, intentionally, and strategically.

By the end of the first year, the improbable possibility of a church built on the simple foundations of Jesus, the Bible, and authenticity was shaping into a reality. I was still exhausted and hadn't made a dime from our church, but people were getting saved and God was on the move. I never could have imagined or expected anything more.

WHAT WE LEARNED-

Don't do too much too fast.

The old adage, "The Tortoise always beats the Hare" holds true in starting a church. Far too many leaders in young churches try to start off with multiple volunteer teams, programs, services, and ministries only to realize that they don't really have the time, personnel, facilities, and budget to do any of them well. Focus on doing *one thing excellently* before you add another ministry or program. For us during that first year, it was our Sunday service. When we tried to branch out and do a small group before we were ready, we ended up launching it without the right person at the helm (remember the pot smoking Ezekiel study?) and had a huge mess to clean up. Be patient and focus on doing something excellently before you try to start up anything else.

Stay as simple as possible for as long as possible

The natural tendency in any organization (but especially a church) is to gravitate towards complexity. Many young churches have the best of intentions in wanting to start off organized, so they create multiple ministries, mid-week services, org charts, committees, policies, leadership positions, decision-making processes, doctrinal stances, and church distinctives all pre-maturely. Those things are great and your church needs them, but at the beginning stages of your church, all of those things need to be exceptionally flexible. They will all change because your church will change as you grow. I think it was Peter Drucker that said, "Culture eats strategy for breakfast". What he meant by that is the culture you create as a church will drive your strategies, not the other way around. So focus on creating a culture of simplicity centered on your values. Keep it simple. All the other stuff will come eventually as you grow.

Don't shuffle Christians, focus on the lost

We live in a city just outside of Nashville, Tennessee (home of LifeWay publishing, numerous Christian recording artists and record labels, and way too many churches). Because there are so many churches and a

Authentic Pursuit: Building a Church from Nothing

seemingly vibrant Christian subculture, church "growth" in our region can sometimes not be growth at all. Sometimes it's just other Christians coming from other churches. Granted, sometimes it's believers that came from a dysfunctional, unhealthy, spiritually dead church that need to be fed, shepherded, and cared for, but sometimes it's just people who are dissatisfied with their current church experience and want your church to give them what they want- be it a different worship style, better kid's ministry, a more accessible pastor, etc. So the *Church* (the big Church with a capital C) isn't actually growing, it's just shuffling members between local assemblies. Here's why it's frustrating to have a lot of those types in your church- they complain a lot, they're always threatening to leave if you do something they don't like, and they usually don't last long because a newer, better, shinier church always comes along right when you need them to commit. So here's what we learned- those types will always be around and they're always welcome in our services, but we want to focus on reaching the people who don't know Jesus, have never really heard the Gospel, and have never truly been a part of a local church. The majority of our outreach is focused on the lost. We don't want to steal people from other churches. For that reason, we do a lot of our promotion via publications and in places where Christians aren't likely to hang out (like our print ad in the Murfreesboro Pulse next to articles about music festivals and tattoo shops or our outreach to the homeless in a local park). Irreligious people felt comfortable around Jesus, and He spent a lot of time going after them. We want to go after them too. It's also been our experience that when God radically saves someone from a life of sin and darkness, they're usually "all in". Those are the types of people who have been instrumental in building our church. Those are the types of people you want for your church too.

Walk towards the messes, not away from them.

In his book, "Deep and Wide", Andy Stanley talks about walking towards the messy parts of ministry, not away from them. In the early stages of your church, it is critical that you as a leader engage head-on the messy areas of your church that need strong leadership. As a non-denominational church, we had a lot of people show up in the early days with different theological and doctrinal stances, some of which were remnants of whatever church tradition they had been familiar with, and some of which were un-Biblical and flat-out dangerous. It was exceptionally critical for church leadership in the early days to take definitive stances on areas of doctrine and theology that are aligned with Scripture and to have the boldness to call out someone who is teaching false doctrine or not leading in alignment with Scripture. As difficult as it was to confront the small group leader that was encouraging drug use while studying the Bible, I don't know if we would have made it as a church if I hadn't dealt with it as quickly and firmly as I did. But a mess in ministry doesn't just have to be a pot-smoking small group leader. It can be a gossiper, a worship leader that can't really sing, a Sunday school teacher that's mean to the kids, or a person who wants leadership but has some dangerous theology. Paul said it best in 1 Corinthians 5, "a little leaven leavens the whole lumps". Small messes that aren't dealt with quickly turn into bigger messes that can't be dealt with quickly. So walk towards the messes.

Prayer and the power of the Holy Spirit are necessities.

In anything and everything that you do as a leader in your church, make sure it's done with as much prayer and guidance from the Holy Spirit as humanly possible. As Mark Batterson often says, "We're too busy *not* to pray!" From the sermons you preach, to the decisions you make, to the leaders you choose to appoint within your church, make sure every decision has been prayed through and that you're listening to the Holy Spirit for guidance and direction. A prayerless church is a powerless church. In the book of Acts, we see the early church doing more *praying* than anything else. They prayed more than they strategized, discussed theology, or read books on leadership. And they didn't just pray for a generic and unspecific "blessing on their church". They prayed for boldness in proclaiming the Gospel and for the power of God. Remember, these guys had no idea what they were doing! There weren't any other churches around for them to model! But there they were-day after day, on their faces before God, crying out to Him in desperate humility to show up and do something supernatural in their midst. And God heard their cries and fell on them like a mighty, rushing wind and the Gospel went out into the entire world. Church growth techniques, leadership strategies, processes, and systems aren't necessarily bad- but they're just methods, not replacements for the Holy Spirit! My prayer for the North American church is that we would stop viewing methodologies as our practical saviors and start crying out to God for His power to be the driving force in our churches. If you're not ready to get desperate for more of God's presence so you can be led by His voice, and you just want a book or a conference to tell you what to do, you're not ready to lead His church.

Don't be scared of big decisions. Make them carefully, thoughtfully, prayerfully, and intentionally.

As we mentioned earlier, there is great value in planning, practicing financial wisdom, strategizing, and examining a course of action as a church, but there is also equal danger in moving too slowly and cautiously instead of exploring your options, praying earnestly, discussing the decision with your leadership, and just doing something. Far too many churches lose their momentum because they sit back in cowardice and fear, not believing God's promises for their future, instead of boldly stepping out in faith. So don't be afraid of making big decisions. You don't have to make them at a glacial pace if they're made prayerfully, intentionally, and strategically.

Don't compete or compare your church to others

No matter how far you get in this journey, there will always be a church that appears on the surface to be bigger or seemingly better than yours, but don't let appearances fool you-no matter how far along a church is or how put together they may seem, there are still challenges, messes, difficult people, and obstacles that are unique to every church body. So stop comparing your church to others and stop competing with other churches in your community- you're all on the same team anyway! Don't compare, don't compete- *complement* each other. You have to get to a point where you're comfortable admitting that there are some things other churches do better than yours. You have to get comfortable letting a family go to another church if you know that other church is a better fit for them. The less you focus on what other churches are or aren't doing so that you can beat them at the numbers game, the more you can be freed up to pursue what God wants to do in *your* church. So learn early on how to be faithful carrying out the vision that God has given your church instead of focusing on how it stacks up with others.

Reconcile past mistakes to the best of your ability, and build a church, don't steal one

I promised my old pastor that I would not split his congregation and I kept that word. A true leader will go

Authentic Pursuit: Building a Church from Nothing

out and grow the Kingdom of God, not steal people from other congregations. I also reconciled with him. I called my former pastor after I finished teaching the Book of Genesis and we made amends. I am a firm believer that God will not truly bless a church that divides other churches and is built on rebellion.

CHAPTER 3

HIGHLY IMPROBABLE

"Look at the nations and observe—be utterly astounded! For something is taking place in your days that you will not believe when you hear about it." (Habakkuk 1:5)

Authentic Pursuit: Building a Church from Nothing

The Bible is full of instances where God spoke to people through dreams. Joseph had a dream that got him into trouble with his family, yet God was telling him that he would be the instrument whereby an entire nation would be saved and many would bow down to him. Later, God gave a pagan king a dream of such major significance regarding future events that it propelled Joseph into the palace due to the fact that he was the only one who could properly interpret it. Furthermore, Jacob had a dream at Bethel where God showed him that his descendants would be like the "dust of the earth." These are only a few of the places in Scripture where God gives dreams and visions to people, and when God does, he gives God-sized dreams with God-sized results!

When God called me and my wife to start a church, it seemed to come at a very inconvenient time in our lives. We were working at an affluent denominational church in a great city with a large budget and a great salary package. I was speaking at churches all around the country and making quite a name for myself in student ministry.   We had just purchased a home, started to plan for children, and had strong support from the people in our church. In fact, I was beginning to be groomed to be successor to my pastor and was on track to inherit the church that employed me. All of this would change drastically.

When I finally started to accept the call and launched out to start a church, I began looking for proper resources to get me on the path of planting a healthy church in our city. I bought almost every book I could find on the subject and read them all at least once, some two and three times over trying to make sure I knew all of the most effective plans to implement and get our church running smoothly and efficiently.

There was a huge problem though. Most, if not all, of the books I read only worked if certain elements already existed: you had a tithe-paying team already committed, you had denominational support, you could travel and gain financial backers from other churches, or you were wealthy. I had none of these things going for me. So, I was left with very little useful information from these resources. Don't get me wrong, some information was extremely useful, but overall, if one wanted to start a church from nothing, there were no real resources to help plant the church.

Unfortunately, many of the people that I thought would help backed out and churches that I thought I could count on did not offer their support either. That's the main reason I decided to write this book; to help people like me plant a healthy church with absolutely no outside help other than God.

For those of you reading this right now, believe me, it can be done! If God has called you to do this and if you are doing it for the right reasons, it absolutely can be done. Also, keep in mind that no one formula is the "magic" ingredient to build a successful church. But these tools, plus a total dependence on God, can get you started on building a great, healthy, and growing church. Also remember that God gives each person a

Authentic Pursuit: Building a Church from Nothing

vision that is unique to them. God does not want cookie-cutter counterfeit church plants. He wants you to use your talent and intellect to create Christ-followers in your city. Do not be afraid to be unorthodox and different. As long as you are in the Word of God and seeking His will, methodology can be as unique as your mind will let it be.

What is important to keep in mind as you begin this journey is that the key to your success in starting, growing, and sustaining a church is not you, your talents, or your abilities (although God will use all of those in the process). If it is you, your talents, and your abilities that grow and sustain a church, when you retire, get hit by a bus, or cease to be as effective as you once were, the church will become irrelevant or wither away completely.

But if the power and presence of the living God is the key and cornerstone of everything you do in your church-from its inception, to its growth, to its sustainability- your church's impact will live on long after you are gone. It is imperative before you even begin this journey that you check your motives and your intentions. *Are you looking to build a church that makes Jesus famous? Or are you looking to build a church that makes YOU famous?*

The truth is, Jesus never called us to build fan bases for ourselves. Jesus never commanded any of the 12 apostles to pursue church planting for the sake of fame, power, influence, or reputation. In fact, Jesus actually said something quite the opposite. He said,

45

Authentic Pursuit: Building a Church from Nothing

"You know that the rulers of the Gentiles dominate them, and the men of high position exercise power over them. *It must not be like that among you!*"

(Matthew 20: 25-26, emphasis added)

In other words, Jesus is telling his apostles to get rid of the worldly paradigm of success all together. Success in the world's eyes equals your face on the cover of Fortune 500, a high-rise office with a subservient staff and an assistant that gets you anything you want, a Leer Jet, a couple of extravagant vacations each year, and all the power and influence you could possibly want. As painful as it is to admit, success in the eyes of the church world far too often looks more like the world's view of success than Jesus's view of success. But Jesus says, "It must *not* be like that among you!" He goes on to say,

"Whoever wants to become great among you must be your servant, and whoever wants to be first among you must be your slave; just as the Son of Man did not come to be served, but to serve, and to give His life—a ransom for many."

(Matthew 20:26-28)

Jesus never called us to build a fan base, but he did call us to build disciples of Him by being servants and laying down our lives, and we can only do that when we get out of the way and let his name be the name that's glorified in all of our endeavors. If we take all the credit for any of the victories and successes that God gives us in the process of church planting, we'll start blaming ourselves during the times of difficulty and seasons of refinement. We have to get it in our thick skulls that it's not about us at all- it's all about him. Church was his idea, and every church that is not *HIS* church exclusively isn't really a church at all.

God also calls us to be prepared and to do things with excellence. There is a delicate balance that must be struck between trusting in the Spirit and power of God, and working hard to build an organizational structure that is excellent, professional, and effective.

The danger of swinging too far to one side of the pendulum is that one could herald the values of being "Spirit lead" and organic, and in reality be using that as an excuse to be sloppy, lazy, inconsistent, and unorganized. For many of these types of people, the process of planning and organization feels wrong because it doesn't feel very spiritual, but we have to remember that God is a God of order. All throughout scripture, detailed instructions were given by God to God's people on how he was to be worshipped and how they were to be lead. In other words, God is into the details of church. He likes organization. He invented it. Just look at your cardiovascular or central nervous system! Organization, planning, systems, and processes are vital to the success of your church.

However, swinging to the opposite side of the pendulum is equally as dangerous. Churches can fall into the trap of meticulously planning elaborate processes, services, events, groups, creative campaigns and outreaches months in advance without for once stopping and asking what the Lord would have their churches' ministry look like. Far too often, the plans are made and

God's blessings on those plans are sought retroactively. This is a dangerous pitfall that can lead to a church becoming more of a glorified events center, social club, or concert hall than a body of believers that meet together to seek the face of God and are sent out to fulfill the Great Commission.

Before we go any further, you need to know that what you are stepping into is going to be difficult and is going to cost you more than you ever thought you could give. That's why it is imperative for you to know beyond a shadow of a doubt that you heard from God and that he is calling you into this endeavor. In 1 Peter 1:10, the apostle Peter (someone well acquainted with the practice of church planting) admonishes the believers to, "make every effort to confirm your calling." Tough times will come. There will be seasons in any and every ministry, but especially in church planting, that will leave you wondering if you heard from God at all about what it is you are doing.

We are to know and have a deep confirmation from the Lord that this is what he has asked us to do. We are to ask the Lord to make our true motives, intentions, and desires known to us so that we might examine them and repent of whatever is self-serving.

In the book of Acts, when the first church plant was in its beginning stages, a council of Jewish leaders got together to figure out what to do about this new, unorthodox movement that was turning the world upside down. The apostles of Jesus had been arrested and were on trial for their "crimes" against the religious order of the day. Different witnesses were brought before the council with wild and mystical stories of angels setting people free from prisons and of the Holy Spirit performing signs and wonders and of a Messiah sent from God that was somehow raised from the dead. I can imagine the scene now- the uneducated, common apostles in shackles standing before the great theologians and scholars of the Sanhedrin council, a now perplexed and divided group full of angry, accusatory, and baffled religious leaders. But in the middle of this pandemonium, a teacher of the law named Gamaliel, who was respected and held in high esteem, stands up and delivers a powerful insight.

He says, "In this present case I tell you, keep away from these men and let them alone, *for if this plan or this undertaking is of man, it will fail.*" (Acts 5:38)

I imagine Gamaliel was most likely an older gentleman who had seen many religious "movements" in the years he had been involved in ministry. He probably remembered hearing people talk about Judas Maccabeus as the possible Messiah, or Simon of Peraea (a former slave of Herod the Great who rebelled against the Romans), or even Athronges (a shepherd who claimed to be the Messiah and started a revolt against Herod Archelaus). He'd seen religious movements fronted by a charismatic leader and passionate followers start up with vigor and gusto, only to fall apart years later because they were mere undertakings of man. God was

49

nowhere in the equation. But then Gamaliel makes a profound observation-

"...but if this is of God, *you will not be able to stop them.* You might even be found opposing God!" (Acts 5:39)

In the same way, if your plans to plant a church are your plans and not God's plans, they will fail. It doesn't take a statistician or a church-planting expert to notice that there have been many church plants that have been unsuccessful. On top of that, the research does confirm the fact that many, if not most, new church plants don't end up making it. Depending on which research you read, some studies cite as high as 80% of new church plants fail in the first year. ("Chronicles of Church Planting: 80% failure rate" by Elizabeth D. Rios, which isn't entirely accurate. The actual numbers are a bit more complex, according to a 2007 study conducted by the North American Mission Board).

The odds of failure are high, but that's never stopped any of God's people from doing extraordinary things. The odds of being eaten by lions are high when you've been thrown into a lion's den. The odds of being killed by a giant are high when he's armed with a four-foot sword and you've got a slingshot. Know this- no matter how high the odds for failure may be, if God is with you, nothing can stand against you. If you're setting out to simply follow God's plan for building his church through the power of the Holy Spirit, no one will be able to stop you! In fact, if they try, they might even be found opposing God. Your primary responsibility in this task lies on you making every effort to confirm your calling. Do you know for certain that this is what God wants you to do?

If not, that doesn't make you any less spiritual. It's a noble thing to recognize that God may be calling you to do something different. Listen to what he wants you to do and just obey. *But if God is calling you to do this, get busy spending your life in obedience and sacrifice obeying God. Any other life is a wasted life.*

CHAPTER 4

OH WAIT, WE NEED STRUCTURE!

"Without revelation people run wild, but one who
listens to instruction will be happy."

(Proverbs 29:18)

Year two of the Experience Community was exceptionally different from year one. If we were to compare starting our church to building a house, in year one we drew the blueprints, gathered the building materials, and started work on the foundation. Year two was about establishing a framework that could support the structure we believed God was calling us to build. Sometimes that was tedious, sometimes it didn't feel very spiritual, but we knew it was what God was asking us to do.

At the start of 2010, we were averaging between 60-75 people between our two services, which was considerably more than our original five! It was becoming apparent that it was time to bring some sort of order and structure to this whole thing. A church is no different than a family, a corporation, or any other situation where you have a group of people who meet regularly. There must be structure and organizing principles or there is chaos and confusion. *God is a huge fan of order and structure amongst His people.* All throughout the Bible, God gives us examples to illustrate why organization, delegation, and structure is so unbelievably important.

In Exodus 18, the children of Israel are being led by God through Moses to the Promised Land and things are getting a little chaotic. In fact, Moses' father-in-law,

Authentic Pursuit: Building a Church from Nothing

Jethro notices that Moses is spending every waking moment of his day trying to solve everybody's problems. Jethro says to Moses,

> "What is this thing you're doing for the people? Why are *you alone* sitting as judge, while all the people stand around you from morning until evening?" (vs. 18)

In other words, Jethro is asking Moses, "There's a lot of people here, and you can't do it all yourself. Why haven't you empowered anyone else to help you lead this whole thing?"

Jethro then goes on to issue Moses a strong rebuke when he says,

"What you're doing is not good! You will certainly wear out both yourself and these people who are with you, because the task is too heavy for you. You can't do it alone!" (vs. 17-18)

Did you see that? Jethro is warning Moses about getting burnt out! As much as at times it is harped over too much, burn out among pastors is a dangerous thing that should be guarded against at all costs. In 2010, the New York Times ran an article about pastoral burn out that reported that 40% of pastors and 47% of spouses are suffering from burnout, frantic schedules, and/or unrealistic expectations. According to the article,

"Members of the clergy now suffer from obesity, hypertension and depression at rates higher than most Americans. In the last decade, their use of antidepressants has risen, while their life expectancy has fallen. Many would change jobs if they could."

Authentic Pursuit: Building a Church from Nothing

A key component to the survival of your church and ministry is your ability to delegate responsibilities to qualified, able, Godly leaders within your church. Within the first few years of your church, much of your focus should be on finding key leaders to help you carry the load and share the responsibilities. Trying to do it all on your own will at best lead you to doing everything mediocre and nothing excellent, and at worst to burning out and leaving the ministry altogether.

The story in Exodus 18 then goes on to tell about how Moses and Jethro selected from among the children of Israel-

"...able men, God-fearing, trustworthy, and hating bribes." (vs. 21)

Moses was instructed to carefully select leaders within the ranks of God's people to help him lead. Getting help from Godly, able, trust-worthy men didn't make Moses any less diligent, spiritual, or competent- in fact, it made him more effective because in it he was protected from getting burnt out and he was able to spend the bulk of his time doing only what he could do instead of spending all of his time focusing on the trivial tasks. Moses was instructed to "Place them over the people as commanders of thousands, hundreds, fifties, and tens. They should judge the people at all times. *Then they can bring you every important case but judge every minor case themselves.* In this way you will lighten your load, and they will bear it with you." (vs. 22)

Authentic Pursuit: Building a Church from Nothing

Notice that it was the responsibility of Moses to select, train, and give authority to others in helping him with the work. There is an art and a science behind picking key leaders within your church that is definitely not fool-proof (we'll revisit that later in this chapter). At any rate, the responsibility fell on Moses' shoulders as the leader. God definitely guided the process of appointing leaders (which is why you should always start your search for leaders with a tremendous amount of prayer in asking God to send you leaders), but it didn't "accidentally" happen or fall into his lap. Moses had to keep his eyes open and stay on the lookout for new leaders. Moses had to get proactive at structuring the unstructured.

As organized and "professional" as I thought we were, I made a plethora of mistakes our first year. One mistake that I look back on and try to warn church planters about is the temptation to just let everyone jump into some kind of service or leadership role. When starting a new church, it is easy to get desperate or to just say yes to everything because you fear people leaving your new start up organization. I paid a hefty price for this temptation at least twice the first 2 years of our church. The first time came when one of the couples that was there "helping" us from the beginning wanted to smoke dope with half the church. Yes, we had a church split just several months into planting our church. This would not be the last time this happened. Almost the same thing happened with a worship pastor almost one year later. The point is, I should have vetted people more thoroughly and proposed that they take time (we

Authentic Pursuit: Building a Church from Nothing
do at least 60 days now) to make sure the church is a
good fit for them. In this 2-month span, we also keep a
close eye on them, making sure they are mature enough
in their faith to serve or possibly help lead.

At the beginning of year two, we had outgrown
our basement building off the square and were praying
for a new space. I knew that year it was crucial for us,
especially since we were planning to move into a new
space that would enable more people to come to
church, to be proactive about building on the
theological foundation we had already laid in the
previous year. So in the first part of the year, I started a
sermon series called "Building the Foundations".
Though we rarely do series, the purpose of this was to
re-enforce the foundational doctrinal and theological
truths that we were going to continue building upon as a
church. I preached on the cross, heaven and hell, faith
and works, suffering, worship, and the power of knowing
and sharing one's testimony. It was great for us to
continue to build and articulate our church's theology on
a lot of tough issues that many churchgoers
unfortunately misunderstand.

In March of that year, we heard about a new
building that was for rent not far from where were
already meeting. It was next to a NAPA auto parts store
and was the headquarters for a homeless/low-income
ministry before they moved to a bigger space. I wasn't
sure how much the rent was, but I knew the square
footage seemed like a lot more than we could afford.
Still, I took it before the Lord and asked Him to give us

the building. It seemed like a long shot, but God is more than able in winning long shot victories for us. When I met up with the owner and started touring the building with a guy named Zook that had been at the church for 6 months or so, it was hard not to fall in love with the space. There was a large open room that would be great for a sanctuary, smaller rooms that would function perfectly as classrooms for children's ministry and nursery, and a kitchen space to do potlucks and fellowship dinners.

As I toured the building, I guess my excitement must have been written all over my face because the owner started asking some questions. When I told him we were thinking of using the building for a church, he started asking even more questions about the church and the ministries we were doing. I came to find out that the building owner, Ed Florida, was a devout follower of Jesus who had been faithfully committed to the body of Christ in Murfreesboro for years. We had an awesome conversation about the church, about God, and about all that God was doing in our city. Eventually I asked the million-dollar question- "how much for the space?"

Ed immediately asked me a follow-up question: "Well...what can you afford?"

I wasn't expecting that as a response, but after I regained my composure I gave him an honest answer and he quoted me a price that was unbelievably fair and an absolute answer to prayer. When it came time to sign the lease, our agreement was settled on a handshake, and Ed even footed the bill to turn on the utilities and

Authentic Pursuit: Building a Church from Nothing gave us the first month of rent so we could free up some cash to renovate. I couldn't believe how God had provided.

The new building was definitely an answer to prayer, but with it arose new, unanticipated challenges. When we were in the basement, there wasn't a whole lot we could do to renovate it to make it look like a "church". No matter how much décor or embellishments we added, at the end of the day, it was a basement and everybody that came to our meetings knew it and didn't seem to mind too much. But when God gave us a new building that was a little bit nicer, we came to a crossroads as a church. *We could go all out and invest a lot of our money, time, and resources into transforming our new space into a facility that fit inside the mold of what people expected when they heard the word "church", or we could just keep it simple and challenge people to view the church as something more than just a building.*

For some reason in the American church, buildings and all of the adornments that go with them have become the golden calves of our culture. I heard an older pastor talk recently about meetings he often has over lunch with younger pastors who are just starting churches or ministries. He said that when he asks them about their church, they hardly ever talk about God and what God is doing in their midst. Most of the time they talk mainly about church-growth methods, their budget, and their buildings. Hear me out- none of those things are bad, but those aren't what we're called to worship. A building is just brick and mortar. There's nothing sacred or intrinsically spiritual about having a certain type of building. Most church historians believe that the first century church met mostly in homes and the first church buildings did not start to appear until the early 200's. Yet the early church was remarkably effective. Researcher David Barrett reports that by the year 300, or nine generations after Christ, 10.4% of the world was Christian. The scriptures had been translated into ten languages and more than 410,000, representing one in every 200 believers from the time of Christ, had given their lives as martyrs for the faith. Somehow, all of this was accomplished without church sanctuaries, fellowship halls, and Sunday school classrooms.

So where did our obsession with huge, ornate buildings and worship centers begin? The answer can be traced back to the Roman Emperor Constantine's conversion to Christianity in AD 313.

"Before Constantine's rise to power, Christian worship was relatively informal. Believers met in homes, enjoying what they called "love feasts", the ancient equivalent of a potluck banquet. After a meal, they sang hymns, read Scripture, discussed theology, and shared communion. In rare cases, a gathering of Christians in a tolerant city might dedicate a special room or small building for their meetings, but these were nothing more than ordinary buildings decorated with simple murals. After Constantine's conversion, powerful people brought their former notions of worship with them as they professed belief in Christ and began influencing

Authentic Pursuit: Building a Church from Nothing
Christian communities…Before the rise of Constantine, it was not unusual for believers to commemorate the anniversary of a martyr's death by sharing communion near his or her grave. As Christianity became the religion of the Roman elite, they used their influence to take this practice to a new level. They began erecting buildings dedicated to worship on the sites identified with a martyr's death…within a decade, the *ekklesia* ceased to be a movement. It was no longer an expanding group of people sharing a unique identity and purpose. It had become a location." [1]

As much as modern, young, Protestant, "non-traditional" churches would most certainly never claim an obsession with ornate worship centers or Catholic cathedrals, I think we have our own versions of those floating around in mega-churches around the country. It may not be flying buttresses or stained glass windows, but it may be high-tech lighting systems, elaborate stages outfitted with trusses and backgrounds that correspond with the current sermon series, and digital sound systems. There is something to be said for creating intentional environments within your worship service (we'll get to that later), but as a church planter in your first few years, you have to guard your heart against those things becoming idols.

As easy as it would have been for us to use our new building as an excuse to buy a new PA system, new comfortable chairs, a stage, and a lighting system, I felt compelled by God to not do any of that. With all of the needs in the neighborhoods and community around us, with homelessness and families that were struggling to just make ends meet, it seemed wrong to spend the resources God had given us on things that were so secondary and non-essential. So we decided to paint, knock down a few walls to open some space, buy a few more cheap metal chairs, and keep things the way they were- simple.

A trap I often see young churches and pastors fall into is one of overspending on non-essential items, like soundboards bigger than what they actually need or high-end projectors that they buy in hopes that it will make their young, small church feel a little more established and legit. It's not necessary to have all the bells and whistles that larger churches have, and if pastors will be patient and use their money wisely, they can slowly get more "bells and whistles" as they grow. *Don't get enticed by what mega-churches have; they probably started off small, too. Buying equipment like a mega-church when there aren't even 100 people attending your services is foolish.* It's foolish financially because it's being irresponsible with God's money, but it's also foolish because you're pretending to be something that you're not. In other words, if you're trying to do a service like there are 2,000 people in your sanctuary when there are only 45, things are going to get awkward fast. *It's been our experience that people are attracted to authenticity.* When you're real about who you are, where you are, and who you're not, that's a very appealing quality to people who live in the real world and constantly encounter "fake". Being young and small

Authentic Pursuit: Building a Church from Nothing is attractive to some people. Some people find big, polished, "mega-church" style services intimidating and phony. So just keep it real and keep it simple. If buying a huge sound system you really don't need is going to stretch your budget to its limits, don't buy one. If you're not a mega-church, don't pretend to be one. Simple is not the enemy of excellent. Excellence and simplicity can peacefully co-exist side by side. Just because you are small does not give you a license to be sloppy.

This was also the year we got serious and proactive about our financial systems and philosophies. It is very important to take a Biblical approach when dealing with God's money. Unfortunately, I've encountered many churches that excuse their financial irresponsibility with over-arching statements like, "God will provide" and proceed to make foolish, lavish, and extreme purchases. As church-planters, we certainly should have the confidence that God will provide, but we are also called to be wise stewards with everything God gives.

It's incredibly important to practice financial accountability and transparency. There should never be just one person who is solely responsible for all of the financials in the church. As soon as you can, find a group that is trustworthy and dependable to count and deposit the money that comes in. It is my solid and solemn belief that eventually the pastor of the church should delegate this task to the point where he does not handle the money at all and, in fact, does not know who gives. *In our church, I don't know who gives and it keeps me honest when dealing with people. I never want to practice nepotism or treat someone as second-class because of what they are or aren't able to give.* The only time I check on people's financial giving is for possible hires and elder considerations.

Another element to transparency and accountability is creating and following a monthly budget that you share with the members of your church on a regular basis. For a church to be successful in managing its financial resources, budgets are an absolute necessity. Budgets are a control mechanism. They keep you from over-spending in certain areas and remind you of certain costs in others. But, more than that, budgets are a planning tool and an operational guide to help achieve short and long-range objectives. It is essential within your first few years that you get into the habit of creating a monthly budget that you follow as closely as you can.

I recommend starting with just a monthly budget in the first seasons of your church. Your costs will vary drastically month to month, as will your giving. That's why it's important to re-visit this part of your church's operations every single month at the beginning, and when things become more concrete, you can space out the time to maybe quarterly. Eventually, things will get steadier and you'll be able to set an annual budget, but keep it simple starting out. Be careful though- just because you've written a budget doesn't mean your work is done. Anyone who has done a home budget knows it doesn't mean anything unless everyone agrees to live within its parameters. Financial accountability is

Authentic Pursuit: Building a Church from Nothing

unbelievably important when it comes to budgeting. It may take the form of monthly financial reports given to a church board or a weekly accounting of major income made available each week to your members. However you choose to do it, know that it's incredibly important to have some accountability and transparency. We also believe in "fuzzy budgets." This means that you create wiggle room to spontaneously give to other non-profits or people struggling in your congregation, and to hire new people if you start to have rapid growth.

If people are financially contributing to your church, it is your obligation to show them how every dollar is spent. It's been our experience that many people don't give to churches or non-profits because they have no idea where the money goes and they don't think they can trust the leadership that handles it. But when everything related to the finances is out in the open and people begin to realize that the money they give is going to advance the kingdom of God, they tend to be less fearful about it. We started making our monthly budget available to everyone coming to our church several times a year at our vision services. That kept us honest and kept people in the loop about where we were and what they could expect from us.

In short, there must be extreme pre-cautions taken to make sure we do not deal with money carelessly. Often, it is easy to be casual and negligent when dealing with money that is not your own, but if we want to get theological, *none* of the money we handle is our own. Psalm 24:1 says, "The earth is the Lord's, and everything in it, the world and all who live in it."

If everything on this earth is the Lord's, the money we handle as ministers within the local church belongs to God. When we mishandle or poorly manage that money, I believe we will have to give an account for that before God someday.

Moving into the new space was an exciting time in the life of our new church. For the first time ever, we had space for children and babies to go while their parents attended service. I started teaching the book of James and the practical wisdom of God's word was very healthy for us as a young church. We were growing spiritually, more people were finding Jesus, and things were great in the new space, but as we were growing together and getting settled in our new building, something was amiss with our worship team.

At that time, most of the members on our very small worship team were still in high school or had just graduated. Our worship leader, although married, was a college student not much older than the rest of the team. The music was ok- very trendy, very loud, and very different from what you might find in most churches. Our team was definitely creative, I will give them that. It wasn't unusual for them to write their own music or take secular songs and revamp them to use in our worship services. But that wasn't really the problem. The problem was a report I got from some parents of the kids on the worship team. Apparently, our worship leader had been smoking pot with the different members of his worship team.

Although I thought I had made it abundantly clear that we weren't going to be the church that smoked pot for Jesus, apparently this was still an issue. I had to have a meeting with the worship leader and the worship team and make it clear to them that this wasn't ok, that God made it very clear in His Word that intoxication was a sin, and that we had a huge mission to accomplish of making disciples of Jesus, not sitting around in our parents' garages toking on doobies. They seemed repentant at first, but I started getting the sense that the team didn't share my vision for building a church that made much of Jesus. So I asked them to step down. While it was hard thing to do, it was an easy decision to make. We didn't have a back-up plan and I knew we wouldn't have music for a while, but I also knew the vision and mission of the church was too important to tolerate that kind of sin amongst people I considered leaders. Oddly enough, we grew without even having worship. Please never underestimate the power of passionately teaching the Word of God! Churches can grow, even when they don't have all the bells and whistles (or in our case, even the common simple things we've come to expect).

So we were without a strong leader for our worship team. There were a lot of musicians floating around the church, but at the time I didn't see a strong, spirit-filled leader who would be able to take this team and make it what it needed to be. Just as programs can't be run haphazardly, the people who oversee them can't be chosen that way either. Therefore, it was important to assign people who had a similar mindset and supported the vision of the ministry that I felt God had given to me. If things were to be done decently and in order, I had to have leadership who followed God and believed and supported me as the pastor of this particular fellowship. As the prophet Amos says, "Can two walk together without agreeing to meet?"

The following Sunday after I talked with our worship team was one of our vision services. We had no one to do the music for that Sunday and I wasn't even teaching like I normally do. I was halfway hoping and praying that no one new showed up because I didn't want them to have a bad first impression of our church. Before service that day, as I was greeting everyone in the kitchen and foyer area of the building, I noticed a new couple I had never seen before. I immediately went up and begin talking to them, explaining how the day would be different and apologizing that this had to be their first impression of our church.

As service started and I got up to share the vision of our church, I was nervous they would never come back. I could feel myself boring them to tears as I shared the operations, the budget, and where we felt that God was taking us for the year. What I didn't know was that this couple had just left a church because they felt there was no vision, no financial accountability, and no clear direction for where God was taking them. Throughout that morning, God began moving in their hearts about joining the mission and vision of the Experience. That couple was Josh and Jenni Brooker.

In the weeks following the vision service, I got to know Josh and Jenni quite a bit. We got coffee together on a weekday while I was watching my daughter (who was around 2 years old at the time) and she threw up all over my shirt right when we sat down to talk. They didn't seem too grossed out by it, so that was a good sign. After they had been coming to the church for around a month or so, I found out from someone that Josh knew how to sing and play guitar, so I asked him if he would consider leading worship. He agreed to fill in for a few weeks. After a few weeks of him filling in, I asked him if he would consider leading the team. He said he would.

God had provided a leader for that team. It just goes to show that God will always honor us when we take a stand for Him. If I hadn't had the courage to ask the previous worship leader to step down, Josh would have never been a pastor at the Experience. As church planters, we have to have an uncompromising faith in what God has called us to build and a boldness to follow His vision regardless of what the consequences may be. God will always come through. We just have to stay committed to what it is He's asked us to do.

That summer, we worked through the book of 1 Corinthians. It was so needed for us as a church to see what orderly, God honoring worship looked like and what the church could be and should be. With some ladies in the church offering childcare during our morning service, service projects for our community happening on the weekends, and Josh leading the worship team and recruiting new volunteers, it seemed like more and more people were owning the vision. As we headed into the fall, carrying out the vision started becoming increasingly difficult. For one thing, people weren't tithing. There were a lot of new Christians, college students, and individuals from low-income communities coming to the church. Some of them weren't aware that they needed to give, some of them weren't in any financial position to give, and some of them could give but just didn't want to. With more people coming the expenses were growing, but our income wasn't. Money (or lack thereof) was becoming a problem and a huge stressor on me as the leader of the church. As a young pastor that had been burned by religion, I hated talking about money and wasn't very comfortable asking people to step it up with their giving. But the fact of the matter was that if something didn't change, we couldn't keep going and may even have to shut our doors. Numbers don't lie, and meeting the budget wasn't looking too promising.

That wasn't all. A lot of people loved the fact that we did community service projects, had fellowship events, and were starting to offer childcare on Sunday mornings. They just didn't have any interest in helping with them at all. So it became the same people (like, my wife and I) week after week who were trying to make these ministries happen, and those people were growing tired and desperately needed support. To make matters worse, a very dedicated family that was serving with a lot

Authentic Pursuit: Building a Church from Nothing
of the various ministries left our church after a conflict
with another family. So the few volunteers we had
serving was quickly diminished to an even fewer number.
We were sinking fast.

I felt stuck. On one hand, it was great seeing
different parts of the vision finally being implemented in
our church and community. On the other hand it was
terrible because as much as people enjoyed the benefits
of certain ministries, when push came to shove they
didn't want to contribute to them. They just wanted to
take without giving. One Sunday night after church, I got
a bite to eat with Amber (who was helping lead
community service outreaches) and Josh. I shared with
them my frustration with the overall lack of dedication
and commitment I was noticing within our church. I
shared with them the financial struggles our church was
facing. I laid the ugly truth out for them about the future
of our church if something didn't change.

That night the three of us talked a lot about
where we felt the church was headed and how we could
prevent that disaster from happening. The one thing we
kept coming back to was the idea of vision. Andy Stanley
identifies vision as "a clear mental picture of what could
be, fueled by the conviction that it should be." [2] We had
all sorts of conviction about what our church should be-
that was the whole point of my original 13-page
document that would become the Experience
Community. We had all sorts of Bible stories from the
book of Acts and verses from James about faith being
dead without works that drove us to do what we were

doing week after week for our community. The part where we were a little fuzzy was on casting a clear mental picture of what we could be to the people in the seats. In other words, I hadn't done a great job at showing them *what they could do* to help make the vision happen.

I learned from that season that there is no such thing as over-communication when it comes to the vision of a church. As the church grows, people will come in and people will move out. *Constantly and consistently communicating the direction you're going and what steps people can take to join in is crucial to the success and survival of the vision God gave you.* Visualizing where you want to be is not enough. Visualization is useless without communication, and only through effective, consistent communication can there truly be implementation of the vision.

The next Sunday I preached on sacrifice. I shared my testimony and talked about what God had saved me from. I shared what it had cost my wife and me to leave a very comfortable lifestyle in our denomination to follow Jesus into the scary world of church planting, but our story wasn't really extraordinary and we certainly weren't "super-Christians". Simply following Jesus requires a lifestyle of commitment, dedication, and sacrifice. In other words, the normal Christian life should consist of radical sacrifice. I then challenged my small congregation of 75 or so to follow Jesus by sacrificing their time, money, energy, and life to help make our vision a reality.

I talked about the importance of each one of them tithing and volunteering for our church to be successful.

There wasn't an overnight change or any dramatic epiphanies with the clouds parting and a voice from heaven, but after that Sunday there was definite shift in the culture of our church. It seemed like people started understanding that the ministries our church was trying to offer wouldn't just happen on their own- there needed to be commitment and buy-in on their end to make them happen. We started seeing an increase of giving and more people started stepping up to help out with our events and outreaches.

We also started becoming more structured and consistent on Sundays. As a small Sunday ministry team, we started meeting together before service to pray and go over what the flow of the service would look like, which definitely helped things go smoother. We began starting our services off with a short video, a few quick announcements, an opening prayer, and a time of worship before the teaching of the Word. These were small tweaks to what we were already doing, but they made a huge difference. People started getting used to our service structure and for the first time it looked like we actually knew what we were doing, which made first-time guests a little more comfortable. First-time guests turned into regular attendees and regular attendees started serving and giving, which starting giving us some much needed momentum as we moved into the fall season.

Authentic Pursuit: Building a Church from Nothing

In his book, *Entreleadership*, Dave Ramsey has this to say about momentum- "Focused intensity over time multiplied by God equals unstoppable momentum... What we have discovered is that momentum is not a random lightning strike, but on the contrary it is actually *created*." [3] Here's how that formula worked for us- we got intentional about focusing on a few select areas that needed improvement in our church (in this season, it was a lack of giving, volunteers, and the structure of our services). *Not only did we get focused on those select areas, we got intense in dealing with and improving those areas through action, not just talking about what we wish they'd look like.* Not only did we focus on a few areas with intensity, we stuck with our action plan even when we didn't see immediate improvement or results. We gave it enough time to see if the plan would actually work, but more importantly than any of the other things, we took all of our needs before the Lord and let Him speak to our hearts about where we should go and what we should do. When we received clarity from the Lord about our action steps, we did everything we could to execute the plans we felt like He gave us, having faith to know that if they were indeed His plans, they were *unstoppable*. It says in Scripture "that no purpose of the Lord can be thwarted." (Job 42:2). If that's true (which it is!) we need to have enough boldness and faith to believe it and act on it. If the power of God gets into the equation of a church that is passionate enough about the Gospel to focus their intensity on a few areas over time, unstoppable momentum is an inevitability.

Authentic Pursuit: Building a Church from Nothing

After a season of structuring, tweaking processes, solidifying leadership, and challenging our people to step up their commitment- we started the book of Revelation. With the worship team on board with the vision and solid leadership in place, the dynamic during our Sunday services changed dramatically. Our times of worship started becoming less about trendy music and more about lifting up the name of Jesus and seeking the presence of the one true God. There was truly something remarkable that happened in our midst as we started studying the book of Revelation. It was as if we all stopped seeing Revelation as simply a textbook on eschatology and started seeing the return of Christ as something that was closer than any of us could imagine. There was a sense of urgency and simplicity of mission that we all felt as God started stirring up our hearts to continue to make Him known in our community until every ear heard and every eye saw the majesty and glory of our king.

The Book of Revelation comes with a unique promise in chapter 3: "The one who reads this is blessed, and those who hear the words of this prophecy and keep what is written in it are blessed, because the time is near!" I'm still not quite sure how it happened, but somehow, in that season of us reading and hearing the words of that prophecy and striving to keep what was written in it, we went from 75 people to 150 people. God's Words are always true. He was blessing us far beyond anything we could have hoped for or imagined.

By the end of 2010, 8 months after moving into our new space, we were already close to being out of room.

WHAT WE LEARNED-

Take a smart and wise approach to money.

Paul writes to the Corinthian church in 1 Corinthians 4:2, "It is required of stewards that they be found trustworthy." As the overseers of God's church, we bear an incredible burden to manage the resources God gives us in a responsible manner. I think this is why Paul later wrote to Timothy that a man that doesn't know how to manage his own household (which I think includes his finances) has no business managing a church. In any organization or small business, whether it's a restaurant, bank, or dry-cleaners, poor financial processes and systems will restrict the operations and overall growth of that organization. Even though church is a bit different in other areas, it's not really an exception to the rule. We don't get a free pass for being bad with money just because we're doing Jesus work. Get financial systems, processes, and accountability established as soon as possible. Get a team together of ministry leaders and decide on and follow monthly budgets. Above all else, do not spend money carelessly! You do not need all the bells and whistles immediately. Don't get enticed by mega-church things. Keep it simple and stay conservative.

Strong Leaders = Healthy Teams.

A mistake we made in the early days of the church was giving weak leaders a lot of responsibility over ministry teams they didn't really have the chops (or the right attitude) to manage. We figured that a ministry team without a great leader was better than no team at all, but we learned that the mess created by a dysfunctional ministry team with a poor, flaky leader at the helm is actually much worse than having an absence in a certain area. A ministry team is only as strong and healthy as the leader that is overseeing it. We have a policy now that we don't start new ministries unless God provides us with a spirit-filled, strong, capable leader. Sometimes it leaves us without certain ministries for a season, but we know without a doubt that being patient for God to send us a leader is much better than taking matters into our own hands and appointing one that isn't capable. We have also learned that God answers prayers when we intentionally and specifically ask for Him to send leaders.

Over-communicate the Vision.

Proverbs 29:18 says, "Where there is no vision, the people perish." In other words, we can't expect people to follow us if we're not telling them where we're going, or even worse, we don't know where we're going. As leaders, we are called to carefully listen to God's voice and lean in to what He wants for our church, and then constantly and consistently communicate the direction we're supposed to go and what steps people can take to join in. For example, we've learned that people are more likely to give generously when they know what their money is going towards. Therefore, we make a point to show our budgets during our semi-annual vision services and make our financial statements available. When people see that we have no secrets and we're genuine about using our financial resources wisely, there's buy-in on their part. That same principle applies when recruiting volunteers. When they see a clear picture of what you're asking them to do and that it actually *matters*, they're more likely to sign-up.

Intentionally create momentum.

As mentioned earlier, we believe that momentum is created by "Focused intensity over time multiplied by God" [3]When you get intentional about focusing on a few select areas that need improvement in your church, when you get *intense* in dealing with and improving those areas through action, and when you stick with an action plan even when you don't see immediate improvement or results, you create momentum. Momentum is not something one stumbles into accidentally. You must be moving forward to gain momentum. The tricky thing about momentum is that it requires vision, consistency, patience, and intensity. If you're lacking in any of those areas, you're going to struggle to gain real momentum. However, if you are intentional about putting in the hard work to create momentum, you'll see results.

Make the Gospel the main thing.

Scripture warns us that in the last days people "...will not tolerate sound doctrine, but according to their own desires, will multiply teachers for themselves because they have an itch to hear something new." (2 Timothy 4:3). There is an ever-growing trend in the western church to somehow "soften" the Gospel of Jesus Christ and make it more palatable to the sensitivities of seekers and churchgoers alike, but if the story of a holy and merciful God taking the punishment for our sins and wickedness upon Himself is somehow softened and watered down (with all those parts about "sin", "wrath" and "hell" taken out so people won't feel bad), that's not really "Gospel" at all. The word "Gospel" simply means "good news". It's good news that we're broken, because that means we can stop trying to be good on our own and rest in the completed and finished work of Jesus on the cross. But people will never find that peace if we feed them a cheap substitute that won't save anyone. That kind of cheap and blasphemous distortion might grow "churches" (not the Biblical kind, just the cultural kind), but it won't change lives. So pastors- "*preach the word. Be ready in season and out of season; reprove, rebuke, and exhort, with complete patience and teaching*" (2 Timothy 4:2) Take the high road with how you present this Gospel. Believe it or not, some people are starving to hear it and be transformed by it. Preach the Word.

WORKS CITED-

Curtis, Ken. "A Look at the Early Church". http://www.christianity.com/church/church-history/timeline/1-300/a-look-at-the-early-church-11629559.html

London, H., & Wiseman, N. (1993). *Pastors at risk: Help for pastors, hope for the church*. Wheaton, Ill., USA: Victor Books.

Ramsey, D. (2011). *Entreleadership: 20 years of practical business wisdom from the trenches*. New York: Howard Books.

Stanley, A. (2012). *Deep & wide: Creating churches unchurched people love to attend*. Grand Rapids, Mich.: Zondervan.

Stanley, A. (1999). *Visioneering*. Sisters, Or.: Multnomah.

Vitello, P. (2010, August 1). Taking a Break From the Lord's Work. *The New York Times*.

CHAPTER 5

THIS VISION THING WORKS

"There is profit in all hard work, but endless talk leads only to poverty."

(Proverbs 14:23)

Authentic Pursuit: Building a Church from Nothing

The term "church-growth" can mean any number of things to any number of people. Many people hear that phrase and solely view growth as numerical- more butts in the seats in weekend services. However, I think true growth, the kind of growth that God wants for His church, is not only *quantitative* (dealing with numbers and data which can be measured), it is also *qualitative* (dealing with the overall quality and character of the church). Paul is constantly exhorting the young churches he writes to in his letters to develop faith that has value, character, and substance. To the church in Ephesus, he writes:

"So that we may no longer be children, tossed to and fro by the waves and carried about by every wind of doctrine, by human cunning, by craftiness in deceitful schemes. Rather, speaking the truth in love, we are *to grow up in every way into him* who is the head, into Christ..." (Ephesians 4:14-15)

Here's the ugly truth about the church-growth movement that a lot of people won't admit-quantity often wins over quality almost every time. In other words, there are plenty of absurd and ridiculous things *some pastors are willing to try and there are plenty of clear Biblical stances and practices that some are willing to sacrifice just to get people in the door of the church.* From selling raffle tickets to win a free I-pad, to playing secular pop songs to start off "worship", to dumbing down the teaching so it corresponds with the latest TV series, churches will go to unbelievable lengths in attempts to "grow" quantitatively, while ignoring the overall quality and depth of their members' walks of faith. This is a crude bastardization of what the scriptures say true church growth actually looks like. That's not to say that bringing in elements of culture and using modern examples is wrong, but I feel like we have not given our audiences enough credit. We are teaching adults in the same manner children would have been taught just several decades ago.

It seems to me that even though there was tremendous amount of quantitative growth when the Gospel exploded in the 1st century, the early apostles were bent on the churches they planted being spiritually mature and equipped to do ministry. Church growth that is not *qualitative* along with being *quantitative* may not be actual growth. Not just that, a church that is focused simply on quantity and not quality might not be actually be a church. It might be just a glorified events center that garners a massive gathering of spectators each weekend. We must remember, Jesus didn't call us to simply convert, but to make disciples of Him.

As we entered into our 3rd year as a church, we had some decisions to make about who we were going to be. 140-175 people were coming on a fairly regular basis, and we were running out of room, even though we had only been in our new space for around 8 months. It was encouraging that people were showing up on Sundays, but we knew that there had to be more for us as a church than simply gathering together once a week. We had experienced quantitative growth, and we knew we had to have a space to meet in to keep up with the growth, but we also knew that if we were going to be everything God wanted us to be, we had to grow qualitatively as well.

So in the beginning of our 3rd year, the leadership team of our church took time to intentionally seek the Lord and what His plans were for us as a church through a 40-day fast. We decided that for 40 days we were going to abstain from certain foods, certain drinks (like coffee and sodas), and all media that wasn't Christian. We agreed to use that time to seek God's face for our church and see what His answers would be for our space issue and our need to grow together in our spiritual walks. Around that time, God started doing some incredible things in the hearts of the people in our church.

A group from our church mostly in their early and mid-twenties started noticing that there were a lot of homeless people in our city. Seeing a panhandler near a busy intersection on a bitterly cold wintery day was becoming more of a common occurrence in Murfreesboro, and simply ignoring them and driving past them on the way to church service was becoming more and more difficult because of the conviction from God. The Holy Spirit was working overtime on their hearts to do something for this group of people that our society had pretty much given up on. So this group of young twenty-somethings *decided it was better to just do something than overcomplicate the issue and do nothing*, and decided to make some pancakes on a Sunday morning before church to give away at the park. The first Sunday they made breakfast at the church, their pancake griddle blew a breaker in the building and the worship team didn't have their soundboard for a few minutes until we could find the break box and flip it back on again. When they finally made it out to the park, there were maybe 5-6 people that showed up. Some of them came to church after they ate their pancakes, some didn't, but all of them had a warm meal and the love of Christ shown to them through this weird group of young people. As the weeks went on, 5-6 homeless people turned into 10-12, which turned into 18-20, which eventually grew to 50-60. The group of weird young people grew into an eclectic mix of people from all walks of life that were hungry to show the love of Christ to the least of these. The group attending our Sunday services started looking more and more different and less and less homogenized. It wasn't uncommon to see a homeless person sitting next to a college student or a middle class white family sitting next to an African American family who lived in the housing projects down the street.

Since that day, the 5,000 ministry had fed over 25,000 meals to the homeless and low-income community in our city. We've seen lives changed, families put back together, addictions broken, and the Gospel explode in the lives of so many people that were at one time just nuisances to us on the corners of busy intersections. All because some twenty-somethings heard from God, stopped making excuses and starting making pancakes.

Authentic Pursuit: Building a Church from Nothing

Around that same time, God was speaking to another group in our church about the high school and middle school students in our community. We'd seen a lot of middle and high school students come through the doors of our church, but we had never offered a ministry or service specifically geared towards them. That all started to change when God started to whisper to Cory Drake, a college student who had been coming to the church for about a year, during the fast about doing something for that group of kids. Cory started talking with me and other leaders in the church about what God was doing in Him and speaking to Him, and he couldn't shake off the burden that was weighing heavily on his heart for the students in our church and community. So in the spring of that year, after the fast, Cory started our youth ministry at the Experience Community.

What started as an organic, kind of awkward, crazy group of 10-12 middle/high-schoolers and 2-3 not so confident college students filling in as leaders, has grown into a group of over 150 students and 25 volunteers from all walks of life. Through Encounter student ministries, we've seen hundreds of kids meet Christ, grow in their faith, get set free from identity issues and brokenness, and find a place to belong. All because a college student listened and obeyed the voice of God during a time of seeking and praying.

Those weren't the only miraculous things that happened during the fast. After searching for space downtown for what seemed like months and coming away empty-handed, we learned that the building *right next door* to us, an old abandoned grocery store, had just come up for rent. Not only was it right next door (which seemed like a miracle in and of itself), the space was almost twice as big as what we were already meeting in. We began praying that the rent price was reasonable enough for us to keep renting our existing building so we could use it for children's and student ministries and the new space for a sanctuary. After a lot of prayer, fasting, and talking about it, we made a move to see what the price tag was. The price was very right and extremely do-able. God is good. It's also interesting to note that it was owned by a Muslim family, which gave us an avenue to create some good relationships with people outside of our faith.

It was around that time that God clarified for me what specifically our vision and pursuit of authenticity should like look. In our vision service in the beginning of that year, I shared what I had received as a very profound revelation to the church, who sat unimpressed because of how simplistic and obvious it seemed. However, the vision that God gave me that year has guided our church through the journey of growing into all that we are today. That vision was (and still is) simply this,

"To lead people to Christ through Authentic Worship, Authentic Community, and Authentic Community Service."

That year, I began unpacking and explaining what exactly that would mean for us as a church as we grew into all that God had for us. Here's what I started explaining then that is still at the bedrock of who we are as a church today-

Authentic Worship

As a church, we believe that all worship begins and ends in a genuine encounter with the person and completed work of Jesus Christ. Salvation is not just found in one or two scriptures, but through a personal walk and relationship with Jesus. Therefore, weekend services are not about entertainment. They are not nor will they ever simply be a rock show or a concert. Weekend services are about pursuing genuine and authentic encounters with Jesus.

To that end, we are a community dedicated to Christ's saving Grace, constant repentance, baptism as a symbol and public profession of Christ's work, the indwelling & empowering of the Holy Spirit (the fruit and gifts), and the marriage of faith and works as the evidence of genuine salvation. We believe in the deity of Jesus Christ, the Bible as the inspired word of God, and in the power of the Holy Spirit.

Authentic Community

As a church, we believe that as Christ-followers we are strongest when we are pursuing Christ with other people. If we attempt to live the Christian life apart from intimate and genuine friendship and fellowship, we are more vulnerable to Spiritual attack and prone to deception. We want to move people away from simply sitting in the seats and move them towards fellowship and meaningful community with each other on a consistent basis.

Authentic Pursuit: Building a Church from Nothing

That's why we strive to create an environment in which people are allowed to live transparent lives with one another and are safe to confess failures, struggles, and inconsistencies. We pursue holiness, reward honesty, and shun hypocrisy. But this only happens when we give each other permission to be honest without fear of rejection. In our church now, we encourage all people to move away from simply attending a weekend service and invest heavily in a small group (we call them Life Groups). Life Groups exist to build relationships, discuss and learn the Bible in a small group setting, and give people the opportunity to pursue Christ together as a people united by His Grace.

Authentic Community Service

We do not believe that God saved us, redeemed us, and restored us through such amazing and scandalous grace just so we could sit in a seat on a Sunday morning or drink coffee in someone's living room on a Thursday night. We strongly believe in moving people to a place of active, authentic Christian service in their community and world. As a church, we regularly do this through monthly acts of community service and giving generously to our friends and neighbors.

That year, we pledged that 10% of every dollar given to our church would be given back to Murfreesboro through community service projects, our homeless and low-income ministry, and other non-profit organizations that benefitted the poor and needy in our community. We have since moved that to 20%, with the hopes of increasing that 5% every year until we reach 50% of our finances being given away. *We believe that Jesus has called us as His disciples to clothe, feed, & care for those who are in need. And we believe He wasn't joking, exaggerating, or speaking symbolically.* We believe that He meant it, and as a church, if we weren't *doing it,* we weren't really a church at all.

So this is our vision and our mission as a church. It's not earth shattering or groundbreaking. We feel that it is normal, every-day, basic Church 101. Anytime as a church we start to pursue a new endeavor or ministry, we ask ourselves a simple question-

"Does this align with the vision and mission God gave us?"

If the answer is no, we don't do it.

If the answer is yes, we do it.

It's as simple as that.

After the fast, it seemed like the sky was the limit for where God was going to take us that year. The vision was clear, God was speaking to us and moving in our hearts, and doors were swinging wide open all around us. However, the one part of the vision that we were struggling to get off the ground was the whole "Authentic Community" piece. To me, it seemed so simple. Just get a group of people together after or before service, go to a coffee shop or Waffle House or somebody's living room, talk about Jesus, pray together, do life, and be happy. Easy as that, right?

If you're smirking right about now, it's only because you know how hard small groups are to get right. You might have been in a bad or poorly planned small group or seen one from a distance that you'd never go near because of how awkward it looked. For us, the initial problem with launching small groups was that we didn't really have any *strong* small group leaders. I would have someone come up to me and tell me how much they wanted to lead a small group, so I would announce that a new life group was meeting and we would have sign-ups and a launch date and the whole hoopla that goes with it. And in a few short weeks, that small group would be essentially non-existent because the leader had good intentions but terrible social skills, was a bad discussion facilitator, or a terrible communicator about when, where, and how they were meeting, and so even with our simple yet lofty and ambitious ideals of "Authentic Community", it was proving to be a lot harder than we thought it would be. For those of you with growing churches, I do not recommend a church starting small groups until over 100 adults are attending service (*100 total adults, not including babies, kids, and teens*).

At least the "Authentic Worship" part seemed to be coming together. We were finishing up Revelation and the worship team was growing and getting better every week. More people were coming, which was great, but we were still running out of room. We signed our lease on the new space in March and we were absolutely ecstatic to get into a bigger and better sanctuary that could accommodate more people. At that time, Sundays made us feel like we were sardines packed into our little sanctuary. We made a joke that all were welcome, expect for Fire Marshalls and people from the Codes department. They could go to church somewhere else.

The old grocery store was big, but it was bare. There were concrete floors and huge glass windows that brought in a lot of sunlight, which was great for grocery shopping, but not so great when you're trying to project words on a screen for worship. We had our work cut out for us to transform an old grocery store into a useable space for worship services, but God was good to us and at the right time sent the right people to us to help make the dream a reality. There was Sean, a contractor and carpenter that started coming to our church, saw the new space and figured we could use a dividing wall to create a foyer and keep the light from shining too brightly on people's eyes during service. So we bought the materials, and he built the wall. There was Norman, a quiet electrician who probably would never preach a sermon or lead a worship song, but he knew how to hang track lighting and install dimmer switches. So we bought what he needed, and he hung the lighting. Different men and women from our church began to treat our space like they would their own home, giving generously of their time and talent to make it a meeting place that was welcoming and inviting to people from all walks of life.

Authentic Pursuit: Building a Church from Nothing

After a month or so of cleaning, painting, building, laying carpet and buying and setting up new chairs, our new sanctuary was finally move-in ready. So on the last Sunday in March in 2011, we had our first services in the renovated grocery store. It was a little strange to have that much breathing room and see some empty chairs at first, but it was incredible to see how far God had taken us in our journey into the other side. Our total cost for this build out was around $5000. Around that time, we started studying the book of Genesis. As we studied the creation story and the brilliance of God in His creativity, it was as if something clicked in the hearts and minds of the people in our church.

The epiphany we all seemed to have as we studied God's Word together was this- if the most creative being that has ever existed lives inside of us, why shouldn't we be more creative?

Why was Christian culture trying to compete (and really, always playing catch-up) with "secular" culture? Shouldn't we be *creating* culture?

Why weren't there better "Christian films"?

Why did "Christian music" all sound the same?

Why was "Christian art" something you wouldn't see in an actual art gallery, but only in home décor stores next to the vanilla-scented candles?

We somehow were rocked with the same revelation collectively- if God created everything we see and we were made in His image, and His Spirit lived in us- creativity should be a natural outpouring of our identity as believers.

Around that time, some of the artists in our church started painting huge murals of Biblical scenes on one of the walls in our new worship space as I taught on Sundays. It was a beautiful and fresh expression of worship. We started seeing amazing scenes of creation, redemption, and God's purpose for us being painted before our very eyes as we worshipped and studied God's word together. Since then, creativity has been an integral and essential part of who we are as a body of believers. We believe that growing in creativity and finding innovative ways to communicate the timeless truths of the Gospel are essential to our mission as a church. *The moment we lose creativity is the moment we've lost sight of our purpose.*

As the church was growing and experiencing a fresh sense of identity and purpose, I was still working the night shift part-time at the MAC and not taking much of a salary. This freed us up to be able to give more and to do more, but it was becoming harder for me to do everything myself (especially when we acquired a new building that needed cleanup and set up every week). In June of that year, I hired Josh as a part time staff member (a whopping $300 a month). At the time, he was a high school teacher and he had his summers off, so it was a good fit for him. His responsibilities were leading worship, helping to keep the building clean, and making himself available to meet with people and oversee some of the other volunteers.

Authentic Pursuit: Building a Church from Nothing

With another staff member on board, we were able to grow in what we offered for our people and our community. One of the things we started doing in July of that year was worship nights. The vision was pretty basic and not too groundbreaking. We asked the question- what if we cleared all of the chairs out of the sanctuary, invited as many people in the church and community as possible, and had a night dedicated to worship and prayer for as long as people wanted to stay? The response was overwhelming. Our first worship night ever we had over 200 people from our church and community crowded in our new space, all united by a desire to lift up the name of Jesus in worship and to see His presence in prayer. It was powerful. One of my favorite memories from that first night was when we dimmed down the lights before the evening started, lit some candles, turned on some instrumental music, and had people praying all around the sanctuary as our guests arrived. Just by walking in the room, people were starting to sense the presence of God. As I walked by a row of seats we had set up in the back, I saw one of the guys from our 5,000 ministry shaking and weeping. The night hadn't even started and no one had even spoken the name of Jesus, yet this man felt God in such a way that he was affected physically. I later found out that it was his first time in church.

That night we sang, we praised, we worshipped, we prayed, and we saw God move in the hearts and lives of so many men and women in our church and community. *Real growth* was happening from the inside

Authentic Pursuit: Building a Church from Nothing

out. The church was growing numerically, yes, but more importantly, people were growing. People were coming for more of God and His presence- not for a rock show or a celebrity pastor.

When we hit the 175-225 mark, we started noticing that it was becoming increasingly difficult to connect on a meaningful level with all the new people. When we were smaller, it was easier to spot a new person and make an effort to introduce ourselves and make them feel welcomed. As we got bigger, that was becoming harder to do. Even worse than that, it seemed like some of the newer people were becoming comfortable remaining unnoticed and anonymous, sitting in the back and slipping out right after service ended. I know some of that is natural and to be expected as a church grows, but for a church that had just begun to make such a big deal about pursuing authentic community that just wasn't going to cut it.

So we knew we had to start doing something to plug new people in. More than that, we knew we had to work on developing something that was meaningful to plug them into, because the small groups we had tried to launch earlier in the year just weren't taking off. We came up with an idea for a type of class during the week that was catered just towards newcomers with the intention of introducing and getting them connected to our church on a deeper level. We decided to call it, "Next" and make it a 6-week class that talked about the church and gave some education about who we were, what our beliefs were, and where someone could go after the class ended to stay connected.

The class went well and we ended up seeing some of the members of the class come to faith in Christ. We baptized a few of them during our 2nd worship night in November of that year. The Next class was a step in the right direction for intentionally assimilating people in our church, but we ultimately decided to change the format. Now, the Next class is a one night class that happens once a month and gives people an opportunity to meet the church staff, tour the facility, and hear more about how to get involved in the Experience throughout the week. Instead of using the Next class to teach basic Christian beliefs, we now offer a 4-week course called "Basics" that meets on Sunday afternoons. Offering separate classes allows us to really be intentional about narrowing our focus. Next classes are about meaningfully connecting with newcomers, while the Basics classes are about offering meaningful Biblical teaching to newcomers.

In the fall of that year, God sent us two very spiritually mature, Biblically solid married couples that had an interest in launching small groups. On a Saturday morning in October, we all sat down together and strategized what the small groups at the Experience actually needed to look like. We knew (from trial and error) that small groups just *don't happen*, so we wanted to be intentional about making them truly successful.

We decided that the process for getting involved in a small group at our church needed

97

to be simple, un-intimidating, and purposeful.
With that in mind, we decided that our first small group
would be held at the church on Wednesday nights. All
someone would have to do to join the small group was
show up. We wanted to remove any excuses an
individual might have for not getting plugged into a
small group, so that seemed like a good way to make it
easy. If and when that group grew, we would multiply
into two groups- with one meeting at the church on
Wednesday nights and the other meeting at a home on
a different night of the week. So in December of that
year, we launched our "Life Group Central" on
Wednesday nights. It was a slow start, with not many
showing up at first. But we stuck with it and started
seeing some momentum over time. Since then, dozens
of Life Groups have been launched from our centralized
hub. Life Group Central is now our largest Life Group
(and the easiest one for newcomers to get involved in),
but we offer something for everybody in our pursuit of
authentic community.

By that fall, we were running around 250, but
really only had four part-time staff members: me (Corey),
Amber (who handled community service), Josh, and Paul
(who took over cleaning the facilities for Josh when
school started back). When I say part-time, I was the
highest paid staff member and I made $600 a month.
Another huge mistake I see many new church plants
make is paying people too much too quickly. We ran
over 300 people before I got a full-time salary (that was
only $30,000 a year with no benefits) and 700 people
before we hired our second full-time employee, Josh.

Authentic Pursuit: Building a Church from Nothing
Even though we had a tiny "staff", we had quite a bit of volunteer leaders who had stepped up to serve their church in a variety of ways.

It was at this point I started becoming intentional about investing in the leaders of our church. We really believe that leaders are learners. There are plenty of brilliant, Godly, Spirit-filled leaders that have done and are doing amazing things in the Kingdom of God that have written books and put out teachings on an abundance of subjects related to church leadership. There are also a lot of intelligent leaders in the secular and business world that offer very practical advice on running an organization and creating processes for success in leadership. For any leader or leadership team to not be willing to pick up a book or pop in a DVD or take time to go to a conference is to not make full use of all that's out there that could change the trajectory of your church- which could in turn change your city and world! I don't know why someone wouldn't take advantage of that.

So we started meeting together on Monday nights to talk about all the issues related to how our church was going, to read and discuss good books, to watch leadership DVD's, and to pray together. We also took a group down to Atlanta in October of that year to the Catalyst conference for Christian and church leaders. Some of the teaching/training we went through together as a young "staff" from the Catalyst conference and other leadership teachings laid the foundations for us to become everything we are today. We would come back from the Catalyst conference fired up. We'd have so many ideas, plans and testimonies of what God had done to us and in us during our time together. *It was always so helpful to get fresh perspectives from churches and church leaders who were further along in their journey than we were.* Our leaders always seemed to produce a return on the investment that we put into them. We learned that investing in leaders always pays off.

That fall was full of successes and new ventures, but it wasn't without its tragedies. We had a high-school student in our community who was very closely connected to our church (her boyfriend and she had been attending pretty regularly for a few months) pass away in a tragic car accident. We had never had anything like that happen in our church. We were scared we wouldn't know how to respond or how to give that family the kind of care they needed during a time of unthinkable tragedy like the loss of teenager. But God was with us, and God has a habit of working even the worst situations out for the good of His people. That Sunday morning, many of that girl's friends from her high school came to church for the first time. We were in the book of Genesis, and the lesson I had prepared before I even found out about the accident was in Genesis 50, where Joseph meets his brothers that had sold him into slavery. I talked about the sovereignty of God's plan in midst of ugly and evil situations, and how what Satan means for evil, God can use for good. At the end of that service, the altar was flooded with high-school students who had never been to church coming up for prayer.

Authentic Pursuit: Building a Church from Nothing
That Sunday afternoon, I was asked to speak at this girl's memorial service at a local high school. Over 600 kids packed in the school's auditorium, and I was given the opportunity to share the Gospel of Christ and the hope of resurrected life with them again. God used this tragic situation to bring many to Christ, and some even started coming to our church as a result of that. There's always a bigger plan that what we can see.

By the end of the year, our church income was finally enough for me to start working full-time at the church and taking a very small salary. I didn't have an office (I worked a lot out of Starbucks and other local coffee shops, mainly a cool little place called JoZoara), I was still watching my 2 year daughter during the day, and I didn't have any staff around to work with, but it was a welcome change to working nights at the MAC! It was encouraging to finally see other leaders step up and work alongside of me to do the various ministries and meet the needs within the church.

We ended 2011 running around 300 between the two services. God was truly doing something incredible. We had essentially doubled in one year, something we didn't think we could ever do or would ever do again, oddly enough God did this again in just a couple years. But what was even more incredible than that was the fact that we were beginning to see people genuinely grow in their faith and trust of all that God is. We were seeing leaders groomed and becoming disciples of Jesus. Growth had happened. Real growth, both *quantitative* and *qualitative*. We decided then that if we ever had one without the other, something is amiss. Since that year, we've always sought to hold onto that value. It hasn't been easy and it's always been messy, but maybe that's how discipleship is supposed to be. It was about to get a whole lot messier.

WHAT WE LEARNED-

Never sacrifice outreach for the sake of in-reach

Once your church reaches a decent size and people start coming regularly, the temptation often becomes to focus more on primarily providing service and ministry for the needs of the people *already in your church* rather than keeping an eye on the needs of the people in the community. The "Christian-ese" rhetoric that is often used to justify this disproportionate investment of time, money, facilities, resources, and leadership usually has a lot of do with the word "fellowship". As more people started coming to our church and began seeing us as their church home, we started feeling pressure from some people to offer ministries and services that had more to do with meeting their family's social needs than anything else. Meeting an individual or a family's social needs is not necessarily "bad" in and of itself, but it can quickly realign and hijack the vision of your church. Hear me out- I'm all for fellowship and I think Jesus is too. However, if a church is not careful, it can quickly turn into a glorified events center for Christians (like a VFW hall for Jesus) rather than a ministry center that equips and sends out disciples of Jesus into the darkness.

Authentic Pursuit: Building a Church from Nothing

There are also other people who don't just want a social gathering. There are people who legitimately desire and need discipleship and community in a smaller group setting. That's a valid and reasonable expectation and something a church should be offering if it's being obedient and faithful in truly "equipping the saints", but if we're not careful, this is where some churches can get hung up. There can be a heavy investment of resources (time, money, facilities, and leadership) on "in-reach" through good things (like discipleship classes, spiritual gifts seminars, Sunday school, small groups, etc.) to people who are already plugged into the church *at the expense of doing anything for the people outside of the walls of the church.*

So the church might have a very knowledgeable group of people who can explain penal substitutionary atonement, historicist views of eschatology, and the regulative principle- but have never gone out and fed and clothed the people who are living in poverty in their own communities, or worse yet, even shared the Gospel with them or invited them to church.

We had seen (and even come from) churches that were experts at offering programs and ministries to the people in the church, but had never done any outreach to the people in the community. So we had to decide at the beginning stages of our church that this wasn't going to be us. We drew a line in the sand and decided that we would NEVER sacrifice outreach for in-reach. We would always be proactive about meeting the needs of the people in our community through things like the 5,000 ministry (homeless/low-income), Bar ministry (where we serve water and hotdogs to people coming out of bars on Friday nights), and monthly community service projects. We had to set this in stone early on and make this a disciplined, consistent, and regular part of our vision as a church. We even strive to make sure we don't talk in a way that only communicates with "insiders." When I teach I make sure I clarify Christian terms and teach in a way that is informative to both Believers and non-Believers. We've found that more people are willing to come to church and hear the Gospel when we're willing to go first to them and *be the Gospel.* The old adage is true—people don't care how much you know until they know how much you care.

Never sacrifice in-reach for the sake of outreach

On one hand, we knew we could never sacrifice outreach for the sake of in-reach, but we also knew that we had a responsibility to the people who had made us their church home to disciple, train, mentor, and even provide them with opportunities to "fellowship" (yes, I said it!) and develop community together. It was also a temptation with a young, rapidly growing church to spend most of our time, resources, and attention on all of the new people coming in. There were a lot of people who had been with us since the beginning that started feeling a bit left out and ignored by leadership (and rightly so) as the church started growing. We knew we had to get better at caring for them too, not just the new people and those in the community.

Our Life Groups have been a very effective method to put people in smaller group settings in order to study the Bible together, build relationships, and just do life together. From those groups, we've seen people who were feeling a bit disconnected and lonely find close, strong friendships with other individuals and families that hold them accountable in the pursuit of Christ. We see a lot of pastoral care happen organically out of healthy Life Groups. When a loved one passes away or a kid gets sick or a baby is born- that person's Life Group is usually the first to step up and bring meals or mow the grass or take the kids to school.

It's a beautiful thing to see the body of Christ come together and meet each other's needs through authentic community, but that doesn't usually happen accidentally. It has to developed and fostered. There has to be intentional investments of resources into things like small groups. Healthy small groups and a healthy small group system are *grown over time*- they usually don't start out fully mature, but with patience, lots of prayer, sound Biblical teaching, and a commitment by the church to make "in-reach" (or, authentic community) a priority and value of the church, they can be healthy.

Take a chance and give people a shot to lead

I think it was Wayne Gretzky that said, "You miss 100% of the shots you don't take." In other words, you never have a chance of success if you're not willing to take a risk and if you're not gracious enough with yourself and your team to allow anyone to fail. In the early days of our church, we learned to let people dream big and to pursue innovation and creativity. We had never heard of a church going out to a city square and passing out hotdogs to people coming out of bars to hopefully sober them up and develop relationships that lead to sharing the Gospel, and we weren't sure if it was going to work, but we let the people who had the dream give it a shot and trusted God with the results. Obviously, wisdom and discernment is needed in this area (you have to know someone's character, theology, leadership skills, and integrity before empowering them lead a ministry), but there comes a point in time when you just have to take a risk with some people in letting them lead. We learned that being willing to take calculated risks with certain ministries and people provided us with more opportunities for ministry in areas and demographics we never thought we'd be able to reach. This means as the senior leader of your church, you're going to have to loosen your grip in the reins and let other people drive every once in a while. This means you're going to have to be gracious with people when they fail (notice, I didn't say "if", I said "when"). Discipleship is never sterile. It's always messy, but the opportunities and rewards far outweigh the potential risks. So trust God, follow your gut, and take a calculated risk every now and then.

Invest in the people who have a desire to lead.

Ok, so here's a Bible quiz question for you- where was Jesus when He said, "It is finished?" Our first thought goes to when He was on the cross as He was breathing His last (John 19:30). If you got that right, good job! But also, look at what Jesus prays to the Father in John 17:4,

"I glorified you on earth, having accomplished the work that you gave me to do."

What was that work? If you look through John 17, there are no mentions of the miracles of Jesus or even the healings of Jesus. The work that Jesus says He has accomplished is this-

"I have manifested your name *to the people whom you gave me out of the world.* Yours they were, and you gave them to me, and they have kept your word. Now they know that everything that you have given me is from you. For I have given them the words that you gave me, and they have received them and have come to know in truth that I came from you; and they have believed that you sent me." **(John 17:6-8)**

So what was the work that God the Father gave Jesus to do? It was the work of manifesting the name of God to the 12 disciples. It was the work of showing these 12, blue-collar, uneducated, "rough around the edges" men the character and heart of God and what God's mission looked like on earth. In other words, it was the perfect example of a very loaded term we throw around church all the time, but rarely stop and think about what it actually means. It was *discipleship.*

Discipleship was the work that Jesus accomplished and modeled for us, then commanded us to continue through the Great Commission. Without discipleship, there can be no Gospel Multiplication. The earthly ministry of Jesus was indeed a lot of healing, preaching, and counseling, but it was also spent with Him developing, teaching, and training His disciples. As a pastor, your aim in ministry should be for your ministry to outlive you. If your ministry relies solely on you and your talent, if you get hit by a bus tomorrow, your ministry will be gone too.

It is essential as leaders within the church to be proactive about grooming and developing leaders. When God gives His people the anointing and mantle of ministry, part of that includes developing other leaders. I believe one could argue that if you're not actively developing other leaders, you're not being obedient to the commands and example of Christ to make disciples.

We learned that being proactive about investing in potential leaders always pays off. But not every potential leader you pour into will pan out. Just look at Judas. A lot of the people that approach you with a desire to lead within your church have selfish intentions, many have unrealistic expectations, and some just won't be willing to work hard and follow through. Those people will always be there. That shouldn't stop you from still pouring into and investing in potential future leaders. In the midst of those people your pour into, there will be the few who will stand out. Part of your job of making disciples and developing leaders includes observing those people who "stand out" and taking an active role at developing them even more. The return that you can get from a leader that you developed and groomed within your organization far outweighs the investment that you've put into them.

CHAPTER 6

WE GREW ON PURPOSE

"I planted, Apollos watered, but God gave the growth. So then neither the one who plants nor the one who waters is anything, but only God who gives the growth."

(1 Corinthians 3:6-7)

Authentic Pursuit: Building a Church from Nothing

We have a simple vision: Authentic Worship, Authentic Community, Authentic Community Service. It is a very simple three-part vision that encompasses and drives everything that we do at The Experience. As we started growing rapidly in our fourth year as a church, protecting and guarding this vision became more of a challenge than we ever thought it could be.

The start of 2012 saw us running around 300 people between our 11 AM and 6 PM services. Our little renovated grocery store could handle between 150-200 people per service and there were only two toilets in the whole place! When we did communion, half the crowd lined up for the Lord's Supper, the other half lined up to use the restroom, so after 8 months of being at our "new" sanctuary, we were already out of room. After 3 years of having the same conversations and seeing the same trends over and over again in growth spurts, we established the fact that rapid growth was becoming the norm, as was our increasingly unusual demographic of non-believers, young Christians, college students, and homeless/low-income people. Our demographic didn't exactly provide us with hefty budget lines. Getting into a bigger space (after only being in ours for 8 months) or buying land and borrowing money to build a building wasn't really an option for us. So with limited resources, one full time staff member, and an awesome, creative God that was gracious enough to give us everything we needed through His spirit inside us- we had to get innovative about accommodating and handling the rapid growth.

Authentic Pursuit: Building a Church from Nothing

When some people hear about the rapid growth that has happened at our church, they can fall into one of two camps. The first is one that meets our reports of growth with raised eyebrows and a look of suspicion. They suspect our "secret" for growth is that we've watered down the Bible, focused on entertainment, or compromised sound doctrine for the sake of relevance. The other is the camp that meets our reports of growth with great excitement and wants to know how they too can grow their church through working overtime to renovate cool hipster buildings, develop sleek processes, and coin radical new ministry philosophies. Truthfully, I can't explain the growth we've had. I think if any of us could, it wouldn't be of God. All I know is that we've tried to be faithful to the vision and mission that God gave us. We've preached the Word, we've fed and clothed our neighbors, we've just been us, and we've never shied away from growth.

Here's a radical idea- I think growth is not only good, it's the point of the ministry. When Jesus commissioned us to make disciples of all nations, to preach the Gospel, to set captives free, and to bring more people into the family of God, this was a call to *grow* the Kingdom of God. Through growing the Kingdom of God, this gives God glory! In Acts 2, rapid growth was the norm for the early church. Acts 2:41 states that in one day, three thousand souls were added to the church in Jerusalem (talk about a growth spurt!). Acts 2:47 states that growth was something that happened on a daily basis.

Authentic Pursuit: Building a Church from Nothing

"...And the Lord added to their number day by day those who were being saved."

Growth in the church looks different in different contexts, but a healthy church will always be a growing church. Listen to what I didn't say- I didn't say that a growing church is a healthy church. There are many toxic, carnal, decadent organizations masquerading as "churches" that are built on cults of personality, entertainment, and false teaching that are growing rapidly. There are other reasons for that (see 2 Timothy 4:3) that are for a future book. I said a healthy church will grow.

So the challenge is this- if true growth (growth of the Kingdom of God through making true disciples of Jesus) is a good thing (and maybe even the point of the great commission), how do we go about welcoming and pursuing it with integrity? We made two observations early on in the life of our church that have stuck with us and been guiding principles for us as we've pursued growth with integrity.

The first is that growth does not have to be coupled with decadence. When I say the word "decadence", I mean just that. Decadence is defined as the "moral or cultural decline as characterized by excessive indulgence in pleasure or luxury." Just because more people are coming and the giving goes up does not mean we should shift the focus towards making people comfortable and pursuing pleasure and luxury above everything else. I've seen way too many

Authentic Pursuit: Building a Church from Nothing churches enter into a moral and cultural decline where they begin to somehow spiritually justify their excessive and irresponsible spending of monetary resources on facilities.

We decided early on that we just weren't going down that road. A practical example for us were church chairs. We had been using black, metal folding chairs since the beginning stages of the church. They were durable, simple, easy to set up, and very affordable, but they weren't very comfortable. We looked into buying cushioned chairs, but a purchase like that would stretch our budget to a point where we'd have to sacrifice doing some of our outreach. As the church started growing, we found ourselves at a crossroads. We could make comfort a priority, or we could keep ministry a priority. We decided that it was far more important for homeless people to be fed than it was for our butts to be comfortable. So we stuck with black, folding, metal chairs until we could truly afford an upgrade. It was a small decision, but one that cemented this value into our consciences. We could grow and still hold onto a mentality of simplicity and frugality.

The second observation we had is that a lot people are actually turned off by the decadence of church. They hear the passages of Scripture where Jesus talks about not storing up treasures in heaven, selling everything and giving to the poor, and at one point even says He doesn't have a home to go to- and then they walk into multi-million dollar mega-plexs of worship with state of the art sound equipment and exorbitant architecture that rivals that of any professional sports stadium. For many people, there arises in them a deep personal conflict. For many of them, that internal monologue goes something like this-

"If these people claim to live for Jesus, follow Jesus, and even work for Jesus- why don't they follow those parts of His teachings? Do they even believe any of this?"

A lot of those people take one look at the excess and come to the conclusion that the church asks for tithes and offerings not so they can do real ministry, but only so they can build more buildings and pay bigger salaries to more rock-star pastors. The seeds of doubt, mistrust, and suspicion are then planted in many of their minds and hearts, and many of them never come back to church. We discovered that many of those in the younger generations (ages 18-35) fell away from church not because they necessarily disagreed with any of the church's teachings, but because they didn't trust the church's leadership due to how resources were used. We decided that we were going to be financially transparent with anyone and everyone who gave to our church and live at a higher standard with how we stewarded the monetary resources that God gave us. We never wanted any of the decisions we made in relation to accommodating and welcoming church growth to give anyone a reason to doubt our intentions as leaders. We wanted to grow with integrity, keeping the main thing the main thing.

After much thought, prayer, and discussion, we arrived at the conclusion that the best way to accommodate the rapid growth in our church was by adding a third service on Sunday mornings at 9 AM. This was going to be a sacrifice for our volunteers (especially those on the worship and hospitality teams), but we knew it would open up some space in our 11 AM service and give us some more room to accommodate all the new people who were coming. In February of 2012, we started our 9 AM services. It was a challenge getting there early, and those first few Sundays were long, but we knew it was the right move. There weren't a lot of people in the seats the first few Sundays, but we gave it time and eventually it filled up. Now, the 9 A.M. is one of our most heavily attended services.

With our growth issues alleviated temporarily, we had more space freed up for another growth spurt, but the ones that started happening in 2012 were different than any that we had previously seen. We began seeing groups of 15-20 people who seemed to already know each other come in together on a Sunday, sit together, and leave right when service ended. They were always friendly and kind, but seemed a bit hesitant to engage in too much conversation or community. I eventually found out that these were groups who had left other churches in town due to a variety of reasons. There was one church in town that closed up shop and shut its doors, so we inherited quite a bit from them. There was another that had gotten a new pastor that not everyone was a huge fan of, so we got a group from them. There were still others that had left churches due to major disagreements with the senior leaders over financial decisions, doctrine, policy, and methodology, and others that had left churches over minor scuffles with other members or leaders. To make matters even more interesting, a lot of the new people coming over were young families with children.

This was all a new trend for us. Up until this point, our church was made up of a lot of people who had really never been in a church and didn't have any preconceived notions or ideas about how church was supposed to be. We weren't very "churchy" (in the summer time, I would teach my lessons barefoot and most times we would start church 5-10 minutes after our advertised time), but most of the people who came didn't know what "churchy" even was. All of the sudden, here we were with an influx of people from other local churches that brought with them expectations (among other things) of how things in churches were supposed to operate.

From this change in demographic, a very healthy motivator was provided to a lot of our volunteer teams to work towards excellence and move away from sloppiness and disorganization. We still encouraged our people to maintain their culture and not change who they were, but we challenged ourselves to up our game at becoming more organized and excellent in areas where unprecedented growth was happening (like nursery and children's ministry). With a sudden influx of new families with young children, a lackadaisical attitude in nursery communicated they we didn't care about them or their children's safety and well being. Little things like a secure nursery sign-in and clean environments back in the children's area became a big deal to us.

The efficiency and flow of our worship services started improving at that time as well. The worship teams were becoming better at picking songs that were easy to sing, flowed together, and went with the lesson I was teaching. More volunteers started stepping up to help with worship and production, and it was an awesome sight to see a diversity of people on stage leading worship that represented all types of people within our church. We had a few guys within our church start making original videos to correspond with the lessons I was teaching and to start off the service. People started looking forward to seeing videos that featured the faces, talents, and voice-overs from people that were sitting in the seats next to them on a Sunday. We were doing our best to maintain our culture of creativity and innovation through mediums that complemented what we were doing on Sunday with excellence.

Our Life Groups were improving and growing rapidly. New groups were starting up and the ones that were already around were growing in community and relationships. We started hearing stories of people coming to Christ and being set free from some pretty serious things through some of the relationships formed and conversations that were happening in Life Groups. Whenever someone new came to the church and wanted to get involved in a smaller setting, we finally had several credible and healthy places and groups to point them to. Our youth group was also growing. Cory Drake was still juggling all of his responsibilities as a college student

Authentic Pursuit: Building a Church from Nothing
and a volunteer student ministries leader, but he was
being proactive about building a group of leaders
around him to help with the responsibilities of caring for
and leading the youth in our church. The Wednesday
night youth gathering became a safe place for a lot of
the kids who had started coming to our church to get fed
spiritually, loved on, and prayed over by leaders that also
had a heart for the authentic.

There was a young man who had been coming to
our church for a while who began to feel a nudge in his
heart to do something for the college students in our
church and community. Murfreesboro is the home of
Middle Tennessee State University, the largest public
university in the state with 25,000 college students. As
our church started growing and more college kids
started coming to the church, we started asking
ourselves what we could do to minister to the needs of
the college students in Murfreesboro. The original vision
this young guy had was for a coffee shop that was open
one night a week where college kids could come
hangout, drink coffee, and discuss the Bible in a context
that would hopefully attract college students who were
non-believers. The idea made sense to us, as it seemed
to meet both the needs of the students who were
already in our church and the needs of those who were
out in the community. On paper, it seemed like the
perfect two-pronged approach- in-reach and outreach.
However, what the coffee shop actually turned into was
very different than how we envisioned and intended at
its inception.

Authentic Pursuit: Building a Church from Nothing

College students started coming, which was great. So at first it seemed like a huge success because attendance was growing, but the more we started looking into who was coming and why they were coming- the more we had to re-examine calling the coffee shop idea a success. A trend that was concerning to us was the fact that many (if not most) of the college students/20-somethings coming to the Thursday night coffee shop were students who were already plugged in at other college ministries in other churches. To them, the college ministry at our church was just another menu item at the church buffet of Murfreesboro. They could go to the college ministry at the Baptist church on Monday nights, the Methodist church on Tuesday nights, the one at the charismatic church on Wednesday nights, and then come to ours on Thursdays. Having college kids go to church a lot seemed like a good problem on the surface, but the real problem was, because they were going to almost ALL of them, they were actually invested in NONE of them. So real discipleship- the kind where deep, covenantal relationships are formed, and accountability and Spiritual growth takes place- wasn't happening. The fact was, a lot of the college ministries weren't actually growing the kingdom- just shuffling around lots of Christian kids who only wanted a place to hang out. What was even unhealthier about this whole situation is that a lot of these church hoppers/college ministry connoisseurs traveled in groups, so it didn't take long for our college ministry to get sub-divided into very exclusive cliques. We didn't know a lot of things about ministry, but we did know that an environment like that

Authentic Pursuit: Building a Church from Nothing didn't align with our vision. Un-churched people could never feel welcomed and comfortable in an environment that treated them like an outsider.

We were at a very difficult crossroads. We had a college ministry that seemed successful (in terms of attendance), but wasn't really being successful at growing the kingdom and aligning to the vision that we felt God gave us. We had a college ministry that was beloved and popular with a very small subset, but ultimately wasn't meeting the needs of the majority of college students in our community. After a lot of prayer, discussion, and strategizing, we made the controversial decision to pull the plug on the coffee shop. We made the decision that we were going to grow intentionally-into who it was we felt God wanted us to be, not sacrificing integrity for numbers or effectiveness for attendance. It was difficult and it garnered criticism, but looking back now we know it was the right decision. It said something about the values of our church.

Crossville, Tennessee is home to the one of the world's largest tree houses. It's actually owned by a pastor named Horace Burgess. The tree house rises 97 feet into the sky, the support provided by a live, 80-foot-tall white oak 12 feet in diameter at its base. Six other trees brace the tower-like fortress. It has some 80+ rooms and dozens of porches, overlooks, nooks and stairways. Built from scrap wood, the site stands in a rural area, but it attracts people from all over the country. What's interesting about Horace Burgess's tree house is that the bottom portion of the tree house is structurally sound, but the higher up you climb into the house's 10 stories, the more rickety and unsafe the tree house gets.

Why? I don't know for certain, but I can speculate. I imagine that over time, people started talking about how the tree house might just be the world's largest. As time went along, I imagine that old Horace started worrying that he might lose that title to someone else. So for the past fourteen years, Minister Burgess has been adding to the tree house using recycled pieces of lumber from garages, storage sheds and barns. The tree house has certainly grown- it's massive (8,000 to 10,000 square feet), but it isn't as structurally sound as it could or should be. It's definitely grown, but there are additions and expansions that don't even look remotely close to the rest of the structure.

Here's my point- if rapid growth (in terms of attendance and size) is all you're after, the additions and expansions you will make to meet that goal can result in unhealthy environments, shallow services, un-engaged attendees, and ineffective ministries. You can grow big and tall without growing strong and sturdy. You can have the appearance of being successful without actually being successful. You can look like you're doing real ministry to grow the Kingdom of God, when in reality you're only shuffling around Christians that just want a place to hangout. Wasn't that Jesus's indictment against the church in Sardis in Revelation 3:2? Listen to the very words of Christ Himself-

"I know your works. You have a reputation of being alive, but you are dead."

Authentic Pursuit: Building a Church from Nothing

Listen- what God really wants for your church is healthy growth. No one wants a house that looks massive but is only one stiff breeze away from a total collapse. In the same way, Jesus doesn't want a church that has the appearance of true growth, but in reality is one unpopular sermon of Biblical truth away from a church split. So make the tough decisions to build your ministries intentionally in the early days of your church. That starts a precedent that will take you a lot farther (in the right direction) than you can possibly imagine.

There's nothing quite like a sudden influx of people from other churches that can cause you to re-examine the values and vision of your own church. With church people comes baggage and sensitive areas from previous hurts in church, as well as expectations of what church "should" look like. After a few months of getting settled into life at the Experience, many of them began to subtly "make suggestions" about how we did things. As I mentioned earlier, many of the suggestions were actually very helpful (like a check-in process in the nursery and kid's areas), but some of them we had to take with a grain of salt. We had someone suggest that we shorten the sermons and focus the lessons around "relevant topics" (instead of books of the Bible, which always struck me as a bit ironic), like money, marriage, and relationships. We heard suggestions about the church hosting more events and conferences, or doing a Wednesday night service, or a doing Christmas Eve service, or the youth group doing more fun nights instead of always being so "serious" (studying the Bible and praying), or the community service events being more publicized by us wearing t-shirts and taking more pictures and sending them to the local newspapers.

Most of the "suggestions" would start with a compliment of whatever ministry they were directed at, but quickly shift into a subtle criticism, followed up by a swift suggestion of how things could improve if only they were done "the way they did it at my old church" (which we always thought interesting, because they had after all, left their old church over the way things had been done). We always tried to show a lot of grace and be kind to the "suggestion people", but we also started having to learn what it meant to protect the vision of the church.

Many people, either consciously or subconsciously, see young churches as perfect environments to import ideas, visions, and opinions for how church "should" be. While some of those ideas can be helpful, a lot of them are very different from the vision that God gave to the leadership when the church was first planted. A great responsibility is placed on the senior leadership of the church to balance being approachable and open to suggestions while being protective of the God-given mission and vision of the church at the same time.

Some of the people that approach you with occasional suggestions for improvement might have legitimate concerns and criticisms. Those are the kind that are important for you to listen to and consider. But there are other kinds of people who are never quite

Authentic Pursuit: Building a Church from Nothing
happy with how things are being done (no matter what
church they happen to be attending), and they will go to
great lengths to make sure the people in key positions of
leadership know it. The truth is, you're never going to
please those types of people. No matter if you're
knocking it out of the park in every area of your church
week after week, there will always be people that wish
you did things differently. In his book Sticky Teams:
Keeping Your Leadership Team and Staff on the Same
Page, Pastor Larry Osborne refers to these types of
people as "squeaky wheels". He says this about squeaky
wheels:

"The natural response of most leaders and
leadership teams is to oil these squeaky wheels. We alter
our plans or give these folks extra attention in the hope
of silencing their criticism. Unfortunately, it seldom
works. Most squeaky wheels keep right on squeaking, for
one simple reason: they don't squeak for a lack of oil;
they squeak because it's their nature to squeak. Wise
pastors and leadership teams know an important
paradigm of leadership: church harmony is inversely
related to the amount of time spent oiling squeaky
wheels."

We knew if we spent time "oiling the squeaky
wheels", we would end up compromising the vision of
the church. So we listened to the legitimate, helpful
suggestions, let the squeaky wheels keep right on
squeaking (some of them right out the door of our
church), and took great pains to re-define, clarify, and
solidify our vision to everyone who was now attending

our young church. I paid a young lady in our church to paint in huge block letters the three phrases of our vision statement on the wall of the sanctuary:

"AUTHENTIC WORSHIP, AUTHENTIC COMMUNITY, AUTHENTIC COMMUNITY SERVICE."

During my lessons, I would frequently make references to our vision and the direction I felt like God was taking our church. I reminded everyone in the seats that if any ministry, program, event, service, or process didn't line up with this vision, we just weren't going to do it. Some of the squeaky wheels didn't like this too much, but most of the people in our growing church appreciated the clarity I gave them on our vision and why we did things the way we did them. Vision services are also a very helpful tool in outlining to everyone who we are, where we are going, and what we are going to do to get there. After that first big influx of church people and the subsequent attempts to import different visions into our church, we started making vision services high priority, non-negotiable items on our calendar. I believe that regularly doing vision services keeps everyone on the same page in terms of organizational and methodological clarity. We always do a vision service at the beginning of the year in January and then another one at the start of the school year (which are usually right in the middle of our two biggest growth seasons).

As more people kept coming and we worked hard to maintain and solidify our vision and culture, God kept giving and sending us "unique" opportunities to help us remember the kinds of people to which we had been commissioned to minister and serve. One such individual was a rather intimidating looking man in his early 60's with broad, strong shoulders that first wandered into our church during a community service event we did in December of the previous year. Right off the bat, we knew something was a little off with him. For one thing, he had different voices, personas, and accents he would switch between at seemingly random intervals. He would find a seat near the front of the sanctuary and often sit and talk to himself as the service was going on.

The first Sunday he was there, I said something during one of my lessons that apparently upset him. He stood up, muttered something nonsensical in a gruff, angry German accent, and stormed out of the sanctuary, causing quite a scene. No one really knew what to say or do. Some of the volunteers from the 5,000 ministry found him in the parking lot and tried talking to him about what he found so upsetting. He introduced himself as Morris. He then ranted and raved for a good 10 minutes about topics ranging from government conspiracies to the apparent healing power of herbs, spices, and mirrors, switching his personas from the angry German to a London chap, then finally to a charming, southern Mississippi gentleman. No one knew quite what to make of it, but everyone pretty much agreed that while he was definitely crazy, he didn't seem to pose any real threats of danger. At this point, we were faced with another decision, a decision that had more to do with our culture and our identity than anything else.

Authentic Pursuit: Building a Church from Nothing

We always had said we were going to be a church for people who wouldn't be accepted in most churches. We had always said that we would be welcoming to the "fringe" people that we believe Jesus loves and died for- the broken, the poor, the sexually confused, the cynics, the atheists, the artists, the addicts, and even the mentally ill. But here we were with a huge influx of "church people", and most of them were white, middle-class families with kids who didn't seem entirely comfortable around people like that. The following Monday night, our leadership got together and talked about what we should do. We all agreed that this guy was definitely going to be a huge challenge, but he wasn't dangerous, he wasn't breaking any laws, and he seemed to have real and legitimate physical, psychological, and spiritual needs. We couldn't just kick him out of our church or keep him out of our services because he made some people uncomfortable. As we talked and prayed about what to do, I started to get the feeling that Morris was a test from the Lord- a test to see if we were going to remain faithful to our vision. I was reminded of the words of James 2-

"My dear brothers and sisters, you are believers in our glorious Lord Jesus Christ. So don't treat some people better than others. Suppose someone comes into your meeting wearing very nice clothes and a gold ring. At the same time a poor person comes in wearing old, dirty clothes. You show special attention to the person wearing nice clothes. You say, "Sit here in this good seat." But you say to the poor person, "Stand there!" or "Sit on the floor by our feet!" Doesn't this show that you think some people are more important than others?

... God chose the poor people in the world to be rich in faith. He chose them to receive the kingdom God promised to those who love him. But you show no respect to those who are poor!" (James 2:1-6)

If we were going to be obedient to God's Word and faithful to the vision God gave us for our church, we were going to have to find a way for our church to be a place for a guy like Morris and for a white, middle-class family at the same time. We couldn't show partiality and refuse to let him worship with us, just because he was a little off and made some people uncomfortable.

So a compromise was reached. Morris was always welcome at our church, so long as we assigned some men from the church to keep an eye on him during the service and escort him out if he happened to get too rowdy (for the sake of safety and not being a distraction during corporate worship). It wasn't pretty, but it worked (for the most part). We figured out that certain words and phrases were triggers to cause Morris to freak out (we couldn't say the word "kids", because he was offended that we would refer to children as "goats"), and there were better ways than others to help him calm down if he got worked up. He also believed the government had poisoned me and was controlling my mind because I had tattoos, and bestowed the title of "minister Joshua" to Josh, recognizing him as the true leader of the church because he thought Josh didn't have any tattoos (for the record, Josh does have tattoos, they just aren't as visible as mine. I threatened on more than one occasion to show them to Morris and expose Josh for what he is).

For better or for worse, Morris was around for most 2012, and our church did a fantastic job at making him welcomed. Ultimately, Morris was assigned to a mental health facility, put on some meds, and got a case manager. He no longer attends our services, but we still see him around town every now and again. Not only that, the small group of guys that started watching over Morris evolved into our security team. They now are responsible for monitoring our facilities and parking lot during our services to make sure everyone and everything is safe. Over the years, the security team at the Experience has been an incredible help to the pastoral staff, monitoring and keeping an eye on unpredictable situations- many times without us knowing about it until after the fact. A security team has helped us as we seek to grow intentionally, maintaining the tension of being a church where anyone can feel welcomed and safe.

That year, we sought to maintain our vision of being a church that values authentic worship by putting on three worship nights- one in April, one in August, and one in November. The nights starting taking on a very unique and creative vibe, as the worship and production teams worked together to move all of the chairs out of the sanctuary and transform the space into a completely different atmosphere. Different décor, lighting, and art that corresponded to the theme of the night filled up the

Authentic Pursuit: Building a Church from Nothing
space during the week of worship night as people began
talking with excitement about all that God was going to
do on those nights.

We started making baptisms unique and special
parts of our worship nights, setting up the baptismal
tanks near the front of the room and giving people the
opportunity to respond to Christ at the climax of the
night through baptism. Some of the sweetest moments
of our church have happened during those nights as
people climbed into the waters of baptism, declaring
publically to everyone in attendance that they belong to
Christ. It kept us centered- reminding us that events like
worship nights (and really anything else we did at the
church) aren't about anything other than directing
people to absolute, total, and 100% surrender to Christ.

Baptism is a big deal to us. We believe that it was
a big deal in the early church as well and that it is the
most Biblical response to the Gospel and one's public
profession that they have received Christ. Why else
would Peter command all of those listening to his first
sermon who wanted to respond to Christ in Acts 2 to be
baptized? Why else would Phillip baptize the Ethiopian
eunuch in Acts 8 after he had believed the Gospel?
Why else would Paul baptize the Philippian Jailer in Acts
16 immediately after his conversion? It is certainly
important to make sure someone understands baptism
Biblically before they get baptized, but I think it's also
important for us to keep the process of baptism simple.
Just like it was in the early church. Some disagree
methodologically with how we do baptisms (because we

don't make baptism candidates go through a 6 week class or get on a mic and share their testimony to the whole church before they get dunked), which I get. But as far as we can tell, the early church didn't do those things either. So while those things aren't necessarily bad, we just prefer to follow a different model than those given to us by American Christendom, mainly, what we see in Scripture.

Starting in 2012, we refined our process for baptizing people. The Sundays following worship nights are baptism Sundays. We worship, I teach a lesson on baptism and the Biblical definitions and understanding of it, and we give people the opportunity to get baptized. Anyone wishing to get baptized talks with a member of our prayer team or pastoral staff, who listens to their testimony and profession of faith, explains baptism again, and then prays with the person before they get into the water. Something else we do that may be a bit different compared to other churches is that we allow people besides our pastoral staff to baptize. If someone leads their friend to Christ and has walked alongside them in their journey of accepting and surrendering to Christ, we give them the opportunity to be the one that baptizes. We feel that while this may seem different and radical to modern church tradition, the Biblical model seems to suggest that all disciples of Jesus have the authority to baptize. Why else would Jesus command it to His followers in Matthew 28? The Great Commission of making disciples, teaching them to obey the commands of Jesus, and baptizing them in the name of the Father, Son, and Holy Spirit applies to all followers of Jesus. Not everyone to whom Jesus was speaking would have ended up becoming a pastor.

Holding to the value of authentic community service in our church means that the desire of God for each of His children is to actively participate in His mission on the earth. We want to grow an army that goes out into the community as the hands and feet of Jesus, not simply a group of spectators that warms seats on a Sunday morning and watches the "professionals" (the pastors and staff) do all of the ministry.

That year we added foreign missions to our ongoing local missions efforts, sending out teams of ordinary people (college students, moms, and businessmen) to the Dominican Republic to work with churches in impoverished areas. We also started making an effort to actively share ministry duties with those who felt called to someday serve in full-time, vocational ministry through a discipleship program called M.I.T. (ministers in training). I met with these guys once a month, read books with them, trained them, prayed with them, and empowered them to do ministry assignments around the church like going on hospital visits and locking up after a service. It was an investment of my time and resources, but most of our church staff came from that first M.I.T. cohort. If I had refused to challenge these guys to step up and fulfill the commands of Christ in the great commission or if I had refused to share any of the ministry duties of the church, I wouldn't have an executive pastor, children's pastor, or youth pastor today.

By the end of year four, we were running close to 500 in all three services. More importantly than that, we had baptized close to a hundred people, worked through the Gospel of John and the book of Malachi, discipled and trained new leaders (who would go on to be future staff), sent out mission teams, and had stayed true to the vision God gave me for building our church into what He wanted it to be.

Growing intentionally is a painful, contentious, often frustrating, uphill battle fraught with obstacles, landmines, and new tensions around every new corner. There were times when the temptation to give in to competing visions from especially vocal parties presented themselves, but in those moments I had to go back to the times when I first heard from God.

Growing intentionally is hard work that takes a rock solid resolve and a high tolerance for pain. God never promised it wouldn't be hard. Only that it would be worth it.

WHAT WE LEARNED-

Grow Intentionally

The question you as a leader should never ask is, "what can we do to grow?" That's what gets churches into doing goofy, Vegas-side show nonsense for the sake of attracting as many people as possible so they can count noses and feign obedience to the Great Commission. The questions should rather be, "what are we doing to prevent God from growing our church?"

Authentic Pursuit: Building a Church from Nothing
and "how can we welcome and pursue growth with
integrity?" I just want to warn you that asking these
questions could be dangerous and shake things up. This
could bring up things you might need to stop doing in
order to welcome and pursue God's plan for growing
your church. This could also expose motives and
intentions in your heart and in the hearts of the leaders in
your church that might not be as pure as you'd like to
imagine.

Listen- America isn't dying for lack of
entertainment. Americans are dying because they're
spiritually impoverished. They need churches- churches
that teach the Word of God and the Gospel of Salvation
with the power and conviction of the Holy Spirit- not
more family event centers for more weekend activities.

If you don't hear anything else from this chapter,
hear this-let God grow your Church into something that
is of quality and integrity. One way to do that is to start
with the end in mind.

Ask yourself- what do you think God wants your
church to be twenty years from now?

No, seriously. Ask the Lord. Stop reading this, ask
Him, and jot some things down.

Now, don't settle for anything less than that.
Don't compromise your vision. Let each stage of growth
in your church be purposeful and of quality. You're called
to make disciples, remember? Not simply Church
attenders. Be patient and wait on the Lord. Don't try to
kick open doors and make things happen that aren't

happening. Grow intentionally by taking small steps in the present to get to where you want to be in the future.

Guard Your Vision

God has a plan and a vision for your church. But so do a lot people of other people that might see your young church as a perfect vehicle to launch their careers and aspirations into full-time ministry, or build it into a place that provides all the ministries they deem important, or to simply turn it into a better version of the church they just left ("old church 2.0").

If new people from other churches start coming into your church, different mentalities, strategies, and methodologies for doing church will get imported into your pre-existing church culture. It is essential for you to reiterate your church's values, vision, and direction on a regular basis. We do this through vision services twice a year and a regular class for newcomers that we hold on the second Monday night of every month (we call it our Next class).

At the Next class, I tell my testimony, the story of the church, and share our church's values and vision. We lay everything out on the table about who we are, who we aren't, where we're going, where we're not going, and what we see as important and unimportant- methodologically, doctrinally, philosophically, and organizationally. We let people ask whatever questions they want and we also have different staff that give tours of our facilities and direct people to what the Next step for getting involved in our church looks like.

Authentic Pursuit: Building a Church from Nothing

Over the years, we've gotten pretty comfortable with sharing our vision and simply inviting people to come along. Our values, vision and mission aren't debatable or up for grabs. If they don't want to come along, we love them, but we're probably not the church for them. There are plenty of good churches around with different ideas and cultures that may suit others better than ours, and over the years, we've grown very comfortable with letting people go instead of trying to adapt, change, and modify our culture in an effort to make them stay.

Honestly and Critically Evaluate Your Success

Your success should be measured and evaluated, not just by the numbers of the butts in the seats- but by the quality of experiences the people in your church are having and the overall depth and strategic success your ministries/programs are having. If a ministry isn't effective, don't be afraid to pull the plug and start over. Carefully vet each ministry and outreach to make sure it is being as effective as it could be.

WORKS CITED-

Massive Tree House in Crosville, Tennessee: The Largest in the World. (n.d.). Retrieved September 22

Osborne, L. (2010). Six Things Every Leadership Team Needs to Know. In Sticky teams: Keeping your leadership team and staff on the same page (pp. 79-80). Grand Rapids, Mich.: Zondervan.

CHAPTER 7

IT HAD BECOME BIGGER THAN ME

"And He personally gave some to be apostles, some prophets, some evangelists, some pastors and teachers, for the training of the saints in the work of ministry, to build up the body of Christ,"

(Ephesians 4:11-12)

139

Authentic Pursuit: Building a Church from Nothing

By the end of year four, we had solidified our vision, we had established our culture, and we had survived a major growth surge without selling out. It was a win for us as a church, but in December we were faced with yet another challenge. We were running around 425 in an old converted grocery store with two toilets. When it was time to take communion at the end of service, half of the people got up to take communion, and the other half got in line for the bathrooms. Not only that, but you could also hear when someone was using the ladies bathroom if you sat on the right side of the sanctuary. We laugh about it now, but the fact of the matter was that we were out of space again. It seemed like in every service we had to pull out more chairs and cram more people into spots where chairs were never intended to go. Parking was a huge issue, and our neighbors started complaining about cars filling up their parking lots on Sundays.

So much of who we are as a church is connected to the culture, feel, and happenings of downtown Murfreesboro. We have the word "community" in our name, so we feel that it's important for us to always remain in the center of our community, staying involved and up to date with what's going on in our city. The old grocery store was in what felt like the perfect spot. I couldn't imagine finding another place that was positioned in a more centralized area that could still meet our needs as a growing congregation. Murfreesboro was growing, the available space off the square was shrinking, and yet, I had a hunch deep in my gut that we were supposed to stay close to downtown. So we started praying.

It can be a daunting thing to look at the current state and reality of your church's situation and know that if God doesn't come through, you're not going anywhere. Here's something I've realized- God's not going to call any of us to do something great for Him that can't be accomplished by His strength in us. When fulfilling the calling of God seems impossible, we have the awesome responsibility and privilege to seek the face of God.

Here's where so many of us get it wrong. We see the challenges ahead of us in growing a church, and instead of seeking the power of the One who spoke the universe into existence- we resort to reading church-growth books, listening to podcasts, and consulting marketing experts to find the latest trick and the "secret sauce." None of those things are wrong, but just think about how ridiculous a trade-off this is. It's like having a fleet of bombers ready to rain down a firestorm of shock-and-awe proportions at any moment, but choosing instead to charge head-on into enemy ranks with a pistol. We have a personal relationship with the God that owns everything, knows everything, and has all the power to do anything on the face of the earth. Not only that, He *invites us, commands us, and entreats us* to ask Him for whatever we need. Sometimes I wonder if one of the reasons we don't see awesome answers to prayer in the American church is because we don't pray with enough desperation and we don't live with enough faith. We don't have enough helplessness in our own efforts and complete dependency on Him to fight the battles for us.

When we look at examples in the Bible of men who did great things for God, we see a completely different perspective. Look at these accounts-

"So he answered me, "This is the word of the LORD to Zerubbabel: *'Not by strength or by might*, but by My Spirit,' says the LORD of Hosts." **Zechariah 4:6**

"*I cannot do it*," Joseph replied to Pharaoh, "but God will give Pharaoh the answer he desires." **Genesis 41:16**

Jonathan said to the attendant who carried his weapons, "Come on, let's cross over to the garrison of these uncircumcised men. Perhaps the LORD will help us. *Nothing can keep the LORD from saving*, whether by many or by few." **1 Samuel 14:6**

Are you there yet? Can you honestly admit, like Joseph, that you *can't do it*? Can you boldly declare in faith, like Jonathan, that *nothing* can keep the Lord from saving?
If God has called you to do something, He's going to give you the things you need to accomplish that task. Trust Him, seek His face and step out in faith. Don't depend on your own efforts, talents, knowledge, skill-set, or abilities. It's NOT about you, it's NEVER been about you, and it never WILL BE about you. It's about

Him. His Church will be built. His Kingdom will come. His Glory will cover the earth as the water covers the seas (Hab. 2:14).

So that's where we were in the beginning of year five. Knowing what God had called us to do, but staring at the impossible- like Moses staring at the waters of the Red Sea, knowing only that God had said, "I'll deliver you". At that point I didn't have an office and I was the only staff member, so I spent a lot of time between appointments and meeting driving around Murfreesboro, looking for available space and praying. On one of the days I was driving and praying, I came across an old factory building that was up for rent just across the train-tracks from the downtown area. It was really old, semi-dilapidated and only half of it was being used as an events center for things like proms and wedding receptions. It was positioned next to a brewery and a bread company and it had a gravel parking lot. It didn't look very "churchy", but then again, neither did the old grocery store. I called the owners and requested a showing.

As I walked into the main room of the building, something told me that this was it. It was a huge, open room with concrete floors, brick walls, white pillars and a high ceiling with wooden beams and windows. It hadn't really been taken care of (there was trash all around and the paint was peeling), but it had good bones. I distinctly remember how trashed this place was. We literally found used underwear from where people had used our now sanctuary as an event center (must have been quite a party!). On the other side of the wall was another 10,000 sq. foot of unfinished space that hadn't been used in a couple of decades- a perfect area for nursery and children's ministry. Above the unfinished space was a large loft area that was only accessible by a ladder and had also been unused for quite some time. It was the perfect size for our student ministry. Everything seemed too good to be true and like a definite answer to prayer- that is, until I inquired about the asking price. The owner was asking $10 a square foot. We could afford it for half that much- *maybe.*

  After the initial showing, I called my leadership team to go through the space together and talk about the possibility of a move. Most of them seemed just as excited as I was when we went through the space together, and just as disappointed as I was when they learned of the price. I can still remember the general feeling of conflicted excitement, nervousness, and hope we all seemed to share that night. Yes, it did seem impossible, seeing an unfinished building that we couldn't really afford. But that night as we prayed together, all of us couldn't help but wonder if this was an opportunity for God to show up and do something miraculous, so that *He got the glory*, not us. I remember one guy saying this was the stupidest move we could make, and though I listened, I knew in my heart what God could do. *As a side note, leaders are often faced with myopic people that can't see the potential of some opportunities. Rise above this and radically pursue what God has led you to do. Don't be an idiot, but think outside of the box.*

We all fasted and prayed for a week or so before I called to set up a meeting with the owner of the building. Before the meeting began, I wrote down on my hand what we could afford to get the space for (around $5 a square foot). I knew that God had called us to be frugal with our resources and not foolish, so if we couldn't get the space at a price that matched our budget, I was going to take that as a closed door from the Lord. I had heard a bit of information about the owner of the building, who also happened to own quite a bit of property and other buildings around Murfreesboro and Rutherford County. I had heard that he was a very influential, successful and also very intimidating man, but I also heard that he was a strong believer and had a heart for the Kingdom of God. As the meeting began, I decided I was just going to be myself and share the story and vision of our church and the things God was doing in us. I also remembered that I had prayed for God to give me favor with powerful and influential people in our city many times. I was once told that if I didn't dress nicer and cover up my tattoos, that I could never have a voice with the more influential and "affluential" of our city.

Integrity, hard work, and just the power of the Holy Spirit can work through any kind of person. I shared our heart for Murfreesboro and how we wanted to stay connected to the downtown area so we could keep meeting the needs of the homeless/low-income community. I talked about the rapid growth we had experienced in the past few years and our vision for growing with integrity and character. As I talked, he listened and wrote down some notes and figures on a notepad. When I finished talking, I wasn't sure what he was going to say next.

I braced myself for bad news as he gave me the price for renting the entire space. I took out my calculator and did some math. The total equaled around $4.25 a square foot, less than half of the original asking price and less than the number I had written on my hand. God had come through and performed a miracle yet again. I've seen it written in the pages of Scripture, but I've also seen it first-hand with my own eyes- nothing is impossible with God.

After collectively feeling the initial shock and elation of getting the space below our asking price, a very sobering thought set in amongst all of us on leadership. We soon would be the tenants of a very large, very old, and very bare, dilapidated building that needed a lot of fixing up. Not only that, but we didn't have the financial resources to just outsource all of the repairs and fixing up that needed to be done in the space. The owners of the building had agreed to help with all of the major build-out needs (HVAC, plumbing, etc.), but for most of the other stuff, we were on our own. After conferring with our leadership team, at our next vision service in January I put out an all-call for volunteers that had experience with framing, dry-wall, painting, electric, and construction to come out on

Saturdays over the course of the next few months to help with the build-out.

   Honestly, that's all it took. So many of the men and women at our church heard the needs and jumped at the opportunity to come out and serve in such a hands-on way. I would like to brag on our congregation. When they heard we would be moving next to a brewery in a low-income area across train tracks from a homeless day shelter, they cheered and clapped. From February to April, almost every Saturday (and even on many week nights), volunteers and the leadership team worked what seemed like around the clock to transform the space into a facility for worship. It was pretty miraculous to witness. Men from the church worked together in crews to frame out what ended up being Sunday school rooms as their wives worked together to patch and paint the sanctuary and future nursery facilities. Youth and college kids gave up their Saturdays to hang out and sweep floors and clean up construction mess. We always ordered Little Caesars pizza for everybody around noon, and people would take breaks and fellowship near the makeshift tables of sawhorses and plywood we set up in what would be the sanctuary. New relationships were formed and existing community was strengthened as we watched the unfinished warehouse space turn into a unique, artistic facility of worship that was unlike anything any of us had ever seen.

   While it was exciting participating in the build-out, it was exhausting. Many of us on leadership (especially me), found ourselves working 7 days a week for two and half months just trying to get the space finished by Resurrection Sunday. A lot of us struggled with staying present with what was happening in the church in the day to day, as it was easy to get lost in what was going to happen next when the facility got finished. *One thing that we learned through that crazy process of building out and moving is the importance of keeping a balanced perspective between the present and the future. Getting too hung up on either one is dangerous, and we learned that in some difficult ways.*

On top of all of the stress and hard work in the week before services began in the new building, on a Saturday as I was working with the volunteer and leadership teams on some of the finishing touches, I got a call telling me that my father had contracted viral meningitis. I had to leave immediately and head up to Nashville where he was hospitalized and in a coma. For a few days, we literally thought he was going to die. I was feeling extremely overwhelmed, shocked, disheartened, and exhausted, but the church came together, lifted my dad up in prayer, and teamed up to finish the space on time. God had brought us this far, and I knew He wasn't going to abandon us. A few days before our first service, my dad came out of the coma and started getting better. God had answered our prayers.

After almost three months of volunteer teams and church leadership working nights and weekends around the clock, the Experience Community had its first Sunday services in the facility at 521 Old Salem Road on March 31, 2013- Easter Sunday. We had a lot of eyes from the community on us during the build-out. You don't hear of a lot of churches renovating an old factory space next door to a brewery with a team made up almost entirely of volunteers from within the church. So the weekend before Easter, the Daily News Journal (our local paper) had done a story on us, advertising our service times and sharing our vision within the community. We knew that because we were in a new space (and it was Easter), we were probably going to get an influx of new people on our first Sunday. We had been running around 425-450 in the month before Easter, so we expected a bit of a boom. Maybe a 50-75 person spike in attendance. But that Sunday, we had 756 people in attendance.

I remember the worship that Sunday. It was so powerful and genuine. The worship team had put together a set of songs that celebrated the resurrection of Christ and the faithfulness of God. The Lord had carried through the entire process of getting the building, building out the space, moving into the space, and sustained us and answered our prayers through all of the difficulty and challenges surrounding those three months. What an awesome God we serve.

Anytime I question the faithfulness of God, all I have to do is walk into our sanctuary. I see the artwork, the décor, and the furniture all built and donated by people within our church. I see the paint colors picked out by some of the women and the walls built by some of the men, and I know that God provides for us what we need and gives us good gifts when we believe on Him to be that provider. When we seek His presence more than we seek His provision, we get more from Him than we could possibly imagine. If God never does anything else for us as a church, He's already done enough to merit everlasting praise. He's given us more than we could possibly ever deserve.

The crazy thing is that the 750 or so people that showed up on Resurrection Sunday (that we thought was a fluke), never really left. Sunday after Sunday, they kept coming, and we really didn't know why, or what to do with them. At this point, we knew we had to step up with providing the new people tangible next steps for getting them involved. Not only that, but I needed some serious help in running the day-to-day operations of the church. I couldn't possibly expect to preach three times each week, do all of the counseling/meeting/pastoring, pay all of the bills, and supervise all of the ministry leaders in a church that was now bigger than any church I had ever even attended (much less worked at). So in May of 2013, I hired Josh as our executive pastor, our first full time hire.

Just for perspective, I didn't work full-time until we had hundreds of people and a second employee didn't come on until we had over 700 people. His job was to help me in the day-to-day operations of the church, pay the bills, oversee the finances, implement the vision, oversee the ministries, and help improve key areas in the church that needed work now that we were bigger.

One of the first projects we took on together was a plan/strategy for assimilating all of the new people at our church into a connected life in our church.

Essentially, we started asking- in our church, how does one go from being a first time guest to becoming an active participant (through groups and service opportunities/volunteer teams)? Are we making those steps clear, simple, and direct? Do people know what to do or where to go next to get involved?

Step one for us meant beefing up our hospitality team. This may seem like a counter-intuitive place to start, but we felt very strongly that the first impression someone gets when they walk into church makes a huge difference in whether or not they decide to come back and get involved. We read a statistic (though I'm not sure where), that the average church attendee decides within the first 11 minutes of being at a church if they're coming back the next week. So it only made sense to us that making someone feel welcomed and invited was critical in assimilating them into the life of the church.

One afternoon Josh and I got out a whiteboard, drew a diagram of the sanctuary, and with X's and O's wrote down where we thought greeters should be strategically positioned. We put some near the main doors, we set some up in the coffee area, and we positioned others near the side doors. We assigned certain hospitality volunteers as "floaters", whose job was to be available at the beginning of service to talk and converse with new people that were sitting in the seats before service (which, in those days was a lot due to our one week, 200 person growth surge). We set up a "connections desk" in the corner of the sanctuary with fliers, literature and general information about Life Groups, community service opportunities, and anything going on in the life of our church. Josh wrote up a "hospitality ministry handbook" and gave it to our hospitality coordinator, Jenny. In it, we outlined exactly what we wanted and didn't want from our hospitality volunteers. All of our hospitality volunteers now have to go through a training that outlines for them our five "big ideas" for hospitality.

They are-

Hospitality is one of the most important ministries of the church.

As the hands and feet of Christ, we are called to serve and reach out to the people in our community. This is especially important when they take the first step in coming to us first. Jesus said that people will know that we are His followers by the way in which we love others (John 13:35). People might not remember sermon details or all the songs we sing in service, but they will remember how they felt when they walked in the building.

We're not (and we never will be) a "McChurch".

As we grow, there is a silent and unspoken expectation because we're in America that as a big church we will afford people the right to convenient, quick, and isolated consumerism ("McWorship w/ a side of McSermon") rather than authentic, deeply committed and intimate community. We must fight this trend on a grass-roots, individual level. Community doesn't just happen- it takes work!

First time guests can be hyper-sensitive, shy and awkward.

Most first time guests will have their guard up, many might be painfully shy and nervous, and some might be going through a serious life crisis that served as a catalyst to get them to church in the first place. Being sensitive to this, but also being relentless in making multiple attempts to connect with them is the only way for a newcomer to feel welcome. Feeling welcome might be a matter of opinion, but no-one should ever leave our church saying, "No-one talked to me".

People can smell phony/fake from a mile away.

Being hospitable is more than the obligatory hand-shake and the generic "welcome to the Lord's house, brother!" It's being genuinely interested in making an authentic connection with a newcomer for the purpose of pointing them to Christ. If you're going through the motions and shaking hands/kissing babies but could care less about actually connecting with any of them, people can tell and it's appalling.

The big "win" for hospitality is a Life Group connection

As a process driven church, we want people to move from Authentic Worship (Sunday services) into Authentic Community (LifeGroups). The "touchdown" for the hospitality team is when someone joins and gets involved in a life group. This should be the big push and the constant campaign that's on the mind and the mouths of all the hospitality volunteers.

Creating a culture of genuine hospitality in your church takes a lot of time, hard work, training, and communication on the part of your leaders. *Even though the church is not a business, there is a lot to learn from restaurants, stores, hotels or theme parks in how they treat guests.* Three companies that we studied in particular were Disney, Chick-fil-A, and Hot Topic (yeah you heard that right). If you've been to any establishment owned by any of those companies, you know how they make you feel as a guest when you walk in. If secular businesses can make someone new feel important and special, why shouldn't the church be top-notch at doing it? We now go so far as to train our hospitality volunteers on conversation starters, making eye contact, and being aware of the people around them who may be sitting by themselves.

We also started announcing and pushing the monthly Next class pretty heavily at this point (announcing it every Sunday), promoting it as the place to go if someone was new to the church or had questions about the church. At every next class, we would heavily promote Life Groups and service opportunities, passing out literature of available Life Groups and service opportunities, with clear, simple, next steps for how to get involved. We changed our Wednesday night Life Group to "Life Group Central" and started announcing it every Sunday. If a first-time guest didn't know where to go for a life group, they could just go to Life Group central on Wednesday night, hear about all of the other life groups that meet throughout the week, and either stay at Life Group Central or go to another life group. We made up "connection cards" that are available to everyone. We now ask first-time guests to fill out connection cards, and then on Mondays we call and e-mail every first time guest to invite them to the Next class and give them additional information about groups and service opportunities.

I know what you may be thinking- "*that all sounds like a lot of work!*" And here's the truth- it is. But for us, it isn't enough to just have butts in the seats. **We want people to be given every opportunity to get fully connected and invested in the life of the church, and we want each step in the process of becoming more connected exceptionally clear and simple.** We've found that the extra effort we put forth in assimilating people into the life of our church pays off with a sense of strong community, a rich culture of discipleship, and an active presence in serving and giving in our community. All of those things are awesome, but they usually don't just happen. You've got to work to strategically build processes, systems, and environments to facilitate those things.

After Josh was hired, we brought on two more full time staff members in Cory Drake as our student pastor (his youth group had recently gone through a huge growth surge as well), and Patrick as our children's pastor. To some people, it may have seemed like I was being haphazard in staffing the church- expending our newfound financial resources that had come with our most recent attendance surge on hiring the closest warm bodies, but nothing could be farther from the truth.

The first three full time hires had been working in their positions as volunteers (or as part-timers) for a couple of years before they came on staff full time. Not only that, all three of those guys had been discipled by me personally through our M.I.T. (Ministers in Training) program. I knew them well, personally, professionally, and spiritually. To other people, it seemed ridiculous and a bit suicidal for me not to hire a staff until we hit the 750 mark, but the truth was, I wanted the right kind of people on my team, not just anybody. To get the right kind of people on my team, I had to wait for certain things to happen for them in their personal lives for them to be ready to take on the responsibilities of full time ministry.

For us a church, getting the right people in the right spots was essential if we were ever going to survive at the pace that we were moving and grow into all that God was calling us to be. In his book, Good to Great, Jim Collins says this about staffing and assembling a high-performing team-

"People are not your most important asset. The right people are…You absolutely must have the discipline not to hire until you find the right people. Good to great companies first got the right people on the bus–and the wrong people off the bus–and then figured out where to drive it."[i]

As difficult as it was to do, I'm glad I waited to hire a full time staff. The men and women we have in the key positions in our church are not just employees- they are leaders of leaders. They possess the right kind of character, creativity, diligence, assertiveness, compassion, initiative, excellence and boldness to solve problems and take on the unique challenges of ministry. They know how to disciple people and raise up leaders under them to make the areas in which they serve excellent. Any employee can make a spreadsheet and sign-up list for nursery volunteers. It takes a true leader to innovate, create, and take the initiative to dream big on cutting edge and effective ministry tools and strategies. Those are the kind of people you want on your team.

For every person that is hired on our staff, whether full or part time, they always have a detailed job description that outlines exactly what we expect from them, what goals we want to see them meet every week, and what behaviors we don't want to see from them. We get very specific too. We learned that there is no such thing as over-communication. If you don't communicate your expectations to the people on your team, you can't get frustrated when they go unmet. So every week at our staff meeting, we go around the table and talk about our weekly goals. Josh writes those down and throughout the week oversees and works with the staff to see them completed. Every six months, Josh and I do staff evaluations, where we go over job performance, job satisfaction, spiritual wellbeing, review goals set six months ago, and set goals for the next six months. We also give our staff permission to speak openly and honestly to us about us as their supervisor/boss. We want our office/staff environment to be as productive, effective, tight-knit, and as Christ-like as possible. For that to happen, we often have to put our egos and our sensitivities aside. It can be challenging, it can be painful, and it doesn't happen overnight, but it's worth fighting for, and it starts with being strategic about communicating expectations.

As our staff grew and we entered into the summer months, I noticed that Josh was struggling to manage all of his responsibilities as an executive pastor and a worship pastor. Not only that, him and I both felt like his long term calling from the Lord was serving more in a pastoral role than a worship role. Over the years I had stayed in touch with my good friend Kyle, who had lead worship for me back when I was a student pastor. I always wondered if there would someday be a place for Kyle at the Experience.

At that time, Kyle was living in Indiana working as an air traffic controller and volunteering as a part-time worship leader at his church, all the while feeling a nudge from God to enter full time ministry. I reached out to Kyle and his wife Rachel, not wanting to pressure them into doing anything that God wasn't calling them to do, but only wanting to see where they were and what they felt like God was asking from them (Kyle doesn't know this, but I always knew he would end up at the church). After a couple of weekends of coming down to

Murfreesboro and having Kyle co-lead worship with Josh, God started confirming in their hearts that they needed to be at the Experience. So they took a huge step of faith, sold their house, packed everything up, and moved down to Murfreesboro so Kyle could join our team. I'm still amazed at their incredible faith at giving everything up to serve the Lord.

God really began blessing the worship ministry at our church when Kyle took over from Josh. As Jim Collins famously says, "the biggest enemy to great is good". Our worship ministry had been good up until that point, but it hadn't been great. Josh hadn't had the time to invest in the musicians, the production teams, and a lot of the technical aspects when he was juggling two job positions. The team began to take on a whole new level of excellence and has risen to a point of greatness. I'd like to think it's because God has honored Kyle's willingness to give up everything in following after Jesus.

By the end of the year, we had hired four full time positions in an executive pastor, a youth pastor, a children's pastor, and a worship pastor; and five part time positions in a missions/outreach coordinator, a production/sound manager, video editor, hospitality coordinator, and a facilities coordinator. While it was exciting and fun to suddenly go from one full staff member to four, rapid growth within a staff can lead to unexpected challenges within the organization. One that we had to manage was making sure our volunteers didn't feel unnecessary. We suddenly went from being a church that was run exclusively by volunteers to having a paid staff that now managed most major responsibilities.

Even though it is inevitable and necessary as a church grows to have full-time, paid staff, the life force of a healthy church will always be volunteers. A highly competent, full-time children's pastor is great, but apart from the 100 or so volunteers that give up their Sundays each and every week, there would be no children's ministry. The same could be said about any and every ministry in our church. That's why we want to constantly foster a culture within our church of outdoing each other in showing honor to the people that serve.

In year five, we knew we had to up our intensity in expressing our appreciation to the people that make our ministries happen each and every week. If it hadn't been for volunteers, we wouldn't even have had a building in which we could do ministry. The hundreds of people that gave up their weeknights, Sundays, and Saturdays so that God's kingdom could be built deserved our gratitude and our honor. So that year, we decided that we were going to go all out and throw a volunteer appreciation banquet- a yearly tradition that has become a favorite around here at Christmas time. We dress up nice, decorate the sanctuary, and for three hours our staff serves dinner to our volunteers, provides entertainment, and gets on the microphone to thank each and every ministry team and volunteer for making things happen. It's definitely an investment on our end (we cater a nice dinner and get gifts for everybody), but it's one worth making to show our gratitude to the people who serve. We've found that when we treat people with value, respect, and honor, like brothers and sisters in the family of God, our effectiveness in ministry increases exponentially across the board. The effectiveness of our church is directly related to the health of our ministry teams. The health of our ministry teams is only as good as the morale of our volunteers. Saying "thank you", recognizing wins, showing appreciation, and developing genuine relationships with the people has taken us as a church to a completely different level. In year five we saw that.

By the end of the year, we had 9 people on staff and around 900 people in the seats on Sundays. For a simple rule of thumb, I think 1% of your church attendance is a good number to have as full-time staff. We'd seen God do a miracle in getting us a new space, keeping His hand on us as we renovated our new space, and going before us as we moved into the new space. We'd seen the Holy Spirit prod and push families to take bold steps of faith, and we'd seen God reward those courageous actions through Spiritual fruit. But the biggest win for us was (and always will be) the number of people that year that responded to Christ through baptism. Around 150 people climbed into the waters of baptism and told everyone in the church that they belonged to Jesus. This remains a measure for us of whether or not we're truly being obedient to the commission of Jesus.

It was a year for the books, and we learned more than we ever thought we could. It was difficult, painful, and it stretched us further than we ever could have imagined- but in our struggles and challenges, our God was victorious. And He always has a funny way of outdoing Himself.

WHAT WE LEARNED-

Communicate and then delegate.

Before I (Josh) came on staff full-time in May, Corey and I spent a lot of time defining my role as executive pastor. We read articles, books, talked a lot, prayed a lot, and even took a field trip to another church to pick the brains of another pastoral team[ii] before writing out job descriptions for both of us. We wanted to make sure we both knew before we started working together exactly what were my responsibilities and what were Corey's. After we started working together, we still kept this practice up- tweaking, refining, and honing our roles as the dynamics of our church and our leadership team changed. We've both found that this kind of communication goes a *long* way in making sure we are effective in our positions. It's our practice now before hiring ANY staff member to (1) determine whether a position is needed, (2) create a detailed (with ALL responsibilities clearly communicated) job description, and (3) over-communicate it to any potential hire that comes on-board our staff.

We didn't do this great in the beginning. We'd throw out very broad requests like "clean the church every week" to the people working for us, not thinking that we needed to specify things like when we wanted it cleaned, how we wanted it cleaned, and any other expectations we had. We found ourselves getting frustrated with staff members over tasks that weren't done to our expectations, and staff members started getting frustrated with us because they didn't know how to work up to our expectations because they didn't know what our expectations actually were. Developing a clear, systematized, on-going process to communicate expectations before delegating responsibilities is essential to the success of any person in a position of leadership.

It's also important to inspect what you expect. Anytime you delegate a duty or task to someone on your staff, the responsibility falls upon you as the senior leader to continuously follow up with them to make sure they know that what you're asking them to do will be monitored. I'm not talking about micro-management (*if you hire the right kind of people, you won't have to micromanage them!*) I'm simply talking about good, old-fashioned accountability. Something as simple as an "around-the-horn" to go over tasks and goals at the beginning of a weekly staff meeting, with another follow up "around-the-horn" staff huddle at the end of the week to check on staff progress of those goals works well. So many issues, conflicts, and misunderstandings within a staff come from a lack of communication and unclear expectations.

Slow walk any hiring process.

The culture of the staff drives the culture of the church. Having a team of enthusiastic, hardworking, friendly, mature, Godly staff members can create unbelievable momentum in shaping the overall culture of your church. On the other hand, it only takes a handful (or even one) of unhealthy, entitled, toxic staff members to negatively influence the culture of a church. For this reason, hiring a staff member at a church should be an incredibly important exercise for any senior leadership team that needs to be walked carefully, slowly, thoughtfully, and prayerfully.

We always want to make sure that any potential staff member at the Experience (1) fills a needed position, (2) has the necessary job skills/qualifications to fill that position, (3) has the proven character, work-ethic, Spiritual maturity to take on the responsibilities of full-time ministry, and (4) has the interpersonal skills to work with a staff and effectively lead team of volunteers. For this reason, we want to do everything we can to truly get to know a potential staff member as much as possible before making any decision to bring them on staff.

We've made mistakes in being far too trusting far too soon, and we've also made mistakes in hiring someone we trust to fill a position that wasn't needed. Both are equally as devastating to the organization and to the individual. Through the years we've realized that a bad hire is a costly mistake that can take *months* (if not years) to correct. What follows is the hiring process we have developed over years of trial and error.

1. Ask, "Do we need a position"? After the Elders and pastoral leadership determine that we do, we

then create a job profile and written job description.

2. Applicant submits a resume and is interviewed by Josh (Executive Pastor). We're looking at strengths, skills, personal testimony, and fit.

3. Interview with Corey, Josh, and the Elders. We're looking for a detailed and well-articulated theological stance, work ethic, and overall fit with the leadership and vision of our church as a whole.

4. Applicant undergoes a final informal interview with Corey and Alicia (Senior Pastor and wife) and the applicant's spouse or family. We get together for dinner or coffee as families. We're looking for family/marital compatibility, personality, cultural dynamics, and overall fit.

5. Joint decision made by Elders and pastoral leadership.

6. Job offer.

Make Systems a Priority.

Up until year five, the way we had done things in our church was very "organic". Things would get done every week before Sunday service- the lyrics for worship would somehow end up on the computer, the communion would somehow get prepared, and the bulletins would somehow get printed out- but they wouldn't always get done at the same time and they wouldn't always get done by the same people. Our service would start with a random video and then some announcements, but sometimes we would mix it up and play a song first or make the video a funny video that had nothing to do with anything. As you can imagine, many times things would be done at the last minute (and there were quite a bit of dropped balls), creating a lot of stress on all of the leaders involved on Sunday mornings. So in year five, we started getting serious about developing **systems** in our operations. In a business sense, a system is a set of detailed methods, procedures and routines created to carry out a specific activity, perform a duty, or solve a problem. In other words, **if there's anything you do on a regular basis that you want the same result for every single time, you need a system.**

For us, we knew early on that anyone that came to us with a request to rent our facility needed to be given the same information every single time. We knew that all of our volunteers across all of our ministries needed to be trained on how to greet first time guests. We couldn't just leave that up to the individual and hope that they were a "people person" and somehow would know just what to say. We needed to take ownership on a managerial and administrative level at communicating exactly what we expected and exactly how certain procedures were going to be done in our church.

All systems that you create for any activity, process or duty need to be documented and communicated before they're implemented. The way we document and communicate most systems across ministries now is through volunteer handbooks (like our hospitality manual) that contain all of the ways we want things done in that particular ministry, and through training/onboarding sessions for new volunteers. For systems on an administrative/office level (like facility requests, staff time off policies, etc.), any new system is documented, communicated at a staff meeting so we can all be on the same page, and implemented immediately. We also have a staff handbook with all relevant systems in it that is given to any new hires. I love how the EMyth Company talks about systems-

"Great systems without documentation are only rumors about the way you do things in your business. A procedure without clear directions is little more than an assumption about the way things should be done. Without documentation, all your tasks, functions, processes, and procedures – the way that you and your staff habitually do everything – are nothing more than good intentions. In other words, you need to write it down. You may want to resist this notion. But how many times have you found yourself telling your employees how to do something? Again, and again, and again?"[iii]

As a pastor/leader within your church, if you have a God-sized, God-given vision and you know how things need to be done on an operational level for all ministries to achieve that vision- the responsibility rests on YOU to communicate that efficiently and to train your people effectively in order to see that vision implemented.

You can't get mad at people who aren't meeting expectations that haven't been communicated, and you can't blame others for not doing their jobs effectively if you haven't done your job at leading, managing, and training them.

So get serious about creating systems[iv]. Here's a snapshot of just some of the systems you might need to have in place across all ministries in your church-

ADMINISTRATION: Annual Calendar, Preaching Calendar, Calendar Request, Counseling Confidentiality Agreement, Counseling Referrals, Event Planning Checklist, Head Count Sheet, Staff Retreat Overview, Statement of Beliefs, Travel Guidelines, Core Values

FACILITIES: Closing Policies and Procedures, Facility Use and Rental Policy, Facility Use Request Form, Building Policies and Procedures, Key and Security System Acknowledgement, Wedding Policies

CHILDREN'S/STUDENT MINISTRY: Children's & Student Volunteer Application, Children's & Student Ministry Volunteer Policies and Procedures, Children's Ministry Parent Handbook, Children's & Student Ministry Philosophy, Background Check policies/procedures

CONNECTIONS/HOSPITALITY: Hospitality handbook, Assimilation Process, Discipleship Process, Baptism Process, Follow-up Baptism Packet, First Time Giver Follow Up Process, First Time Guest Follow Up Process

Authentic Pursuit: Building a Church from Nothing

WORSHIP/PRODUCTION: Service Flow Philosophies, Service Order, Announcements Philosophy, Service Planning Philosophy, Weekend Master Schedule, Worship Leader/Musician Expectations, Audio Production/Lighting Procedures

FINANCIAL: Benevolence Policy, Budgeting Process, Housing Allowance for Pastors, Offering Count Sheets, Reimbursement Form, Spending Procedures, Budget Philosophy

STAFF: 6-Month Evaluation, Blank Housing Allowance Form, Confidentiality Agreement, Employee Handbook, Employee Handbook Agreement, Employment Application, Firing Process, Hiring Process, Interview Questions, New Hire Checklist, Prospective Employee Screening, Resignation Agreement, Social Media Policy, Staff Job Descriptions, Staff Leave Request, Organizational Chart, Termination Agreement

Make Honoring Volunteers a Top Priority

I can't stress how important it is as a pastor or leader to invest in your volunteers and constantly make them feel appreciated for the work they do in your church. Think about this- they work for free, but your church couldn't function without them. In fact, if they all somehow went on strike, the operations of your ministries would go on hold! It is so important that they constantly receive your encouragement, affirmation, support and honor. Don't misunderstand me- we don't honor volunteers so that they'll work for us. This isn't espousing a view of manipulating an army of minion volunteers with empty flattery so that they'll mindlessly perform various tasks for you around your church. That's a weird, Marxist, worker party "strength of the masses" mindset that will get you labeled as a cult leader (and rightly so!).

1 Thessalonians 5:11 says, "Therefore encourage one another and build one another up, just as you are doing." When we are obedient to the scriptures and do this faithfully with those around us and especially to those under our care, we call them out and lift them up for doing amazing things for the kingdom of God, knowing that what is rewarded is repeated. I know in my marriage that my wife's encouragement to me holds much more weight and power than her criticism of me (and mine of her as well). When she tells me "thank you" for doing the dishes with a kiss on the cheek that makes me want to keep doing dishes! I know doing the dishes is important, but now I have an extra incentive to keep doing the work because of that continual encouragement, which feels great. Her encouragement for the work I've done is much more powerful than her criticism for the work I haven't' done. If she nags me because I haven't done the dishes, for whatever reason, I'll put it off until the last minute and then have a bad attitude while doing them. That's just human nature. That's how we're wired.

Over the years I've heard horror stories of churches treating volunteers like factory workers or glorified waiters. I've heard stories of burnout and pastors/staff who are constantly criticizing and never saying thank you. I've heard of dysfunctional teams with internal conflict and power-struggles and people serving together that just flat out don't like each other. And I've met many a believer that loves the Lord and loves the church, but is hesitant to get involved as a volunteer because they're exhausted and have a good image of the church on Sundays but don't want to see the "seedy underbelly" of what happens behind the scenes.

For your volunteers, the research indicates that in order to build a high functioning, high performing team, you should shoot for a 5 to 1 praise to criticism ratio[v]. That means five positive affirmations for every negative comment. The research indicates that in a culture of encouragement, affirmation, and positive feedback, negative feedback goes much further because people understand that they wouldn't be receiving it if it weren't truly needed. In other words, you don't have the right to criticize your volunteers if you aren't first working to encourage and build them up. The vision God has given you for your church cannot be implemented without volunteers, and volunteers will not be all that they can be unless you go out of your way to honor, encourage, support, and build them up on a continual basis.

Here are some ways a pastor/ministry leader/staff member can say thank you to volunteers-

- Words of encouragement/public praise. In a pre-service huddle, recognize someone for their hard work and good attitude. Encourage them publically.

- Encouraging notes/e-mails/texts. Pick someone on a volunteer team and just send them a text one week telling them "thank you" and picking something out about the way that they serve that you appreciate.
- Gifts. Put something in your ministry budget for volunteer appreciation gifts. It doesn't have to be anything huge, but a simple $5 gift card to Starbucks every now and again is a very special way to tell someone how much they're appreciated.
- Quality time. Make time for your volunteers. Take them out to lunch and pick up the tab (put something in your ministry budget for that too!), have them and their spouse over for dinner, go for coffee with them or go to the golf course with them on your day off- all with the agreement that you don't have to talk about ministry (unless they want to). Let them know that you value *them* as a person, not just what they can give to your church.
- Leadership development. Buy the people on your volunteer team a good book on leadership and go over some of it at your next meeting. Invest in them as leaders and build them up as disciples of Christ.
- Appreciation events. Once a year, go all out and throw a volunteer appreciation banquet. Have the pastors and staff serve your volunteers. Dress up, serve good food, give out door prizes, and give out awards. Make it fun, make it meaningful, but above all, make it about showing honor and love to the people on your volunteer teams. For us, this is one of the most fun and special nights of the year.

WORKS CITED

[i] Collins, J. (2001). Good to great: Why some companies make the leap--and others don't. New York, NY: HarperBusiness.
[ii] Alfred Turley and Matt Evans from Rock Bridge Community Church in Dalton, Georgia. You guys helped out tremendously! Thank you!
[iii] Gerber, M. (1995). *The E-myth revisited: Why most small businesses don't work and what to do about it*. New York: CollinsBusiness.
[iv] The Rocket Company (www.rocketcompany.com) has a really cool product called "The Systems Bundle" that has over 200 downloadable documents and forms ready to use or customize for your church. It's a great place to start by using them as a template or a guide. Some systems we've used exactly as they are, but most of them we've tweaked to fit our needs/culture. The product is a bit pricey, but it's an investment that completely revolutionized our operations as a church. Another way to get a jump-start on systems is to sit down with another church staff (one that is ideally further long in their organizational development) and pick their brains on how they do certain processes, procedures, etc. We've found that most churches aren't territorial and usually end up giving us copies of systems and procedural documents that we're more than welcome to add to or tweak.
[v] The Ideal Praise-to-Criticism Ratio. (2013, March 15). Retrieved September 22, 2015.

CHAPTER 8

WHERE DO WE GO FROM HERE?

"But when Jesus overheard what was said, He told the synagogue leader, "Don't be afraid. Only believe."" (Mark 5:36)

"Over 1,000 people came to church this Sunday. Those 1,000 people heard about God. Those 1,000 people heard about Jesus and that He saves. Those 1,000 people heard about a God that heals, about a God that is actively engaged in our day-to-day lives and that hears us when we call to Him.

God, I know this is a milestone...so why do I feel so broken and scared? I feel completely over my head. I feel like if we really have 1,000 people coming to our church then we've had to cheat somehow.

Lord, have we cheated?

Have I been faithful? Have I labored well and trusted You to bring the harvest? Or have we manipulated, coerced and connived to get us to this place? Oh Lord- let us not lose our integrity. Let us not lose our passion. Let us stay true to Your heart and Your will for this church.

God, I'm tired. I'm feeling exceptionally insecure and vulnerable. I don't feel like a pastor. I feel like a charlatan. I feel like a phony. I feel like a little boy who is trying hard to flex his muscles and suck in his gut and pretend to be stronger than he actually is. The truth is, I'm terrified. The truth is, I'm not even sure we're supposed to be here. Yet week after week, moment after moment, you do incredible things in our midst, and it leaves me scratching my head and just leaning on the fact that you've appointed us for these positions.

Let me believe these words:
"I, I am he who comforts you; who are you that you are afraid of man who dies, of the son of man who is made like grass, and have forgotten the Lord, your Maker, who stretched out the heavens and laid the foundations of the earth, and you fear continually all the day because of the wrath of the oppressor, when he sets himself to destroy?...I am the LORD your God, who stirs up the sea so that its waves roar-the LORD of hosts is his name.

And I have put my words in your mouth, and covered you in the shadow of my hand."(Isaiah 51:12-16)

Lord, let us grow with integrity. *I will serve you and say yes to you for as long as there is breath in my lungs. If we're all a bunch of heretics, charlatans, and fools- reveal that to me and show me Your will for my life. I just want You." (Taken from Josh's journal, January 19, 2014)*

I think there's an incredible misconception and naiveté amongst church planters and pastors that I'd like to call the "make-it" myth. This is the myth that says, "When we finally *make it* as a church, it'll all be *smooth sailing!*" **For most pastors and church planters, to "make-it" means reaching a certain attendance** *milestone, finally having a building, or finally having a staff and an organized set of policies/procedures.* No-one really wants to admit it, but they'll look at the lives and operations of mega-churches and mega-church pastors and feel a certain hidden envy for how "simple" and "easy" everything looks on the surface. Once a church has "made it", all insecurity and fear magically vanish from the lives and minds of the pastors. Once a church has "made it", all decisions are easy. Once a church has "made it", there are no longer any conflicts, struggles, or challenges amongst leadership and staff. Everyone becomes spiritually mature overnight, and all people are understanding and gracious...because, after all- you've made it! ...right?

The "make-it" myth is one of the biggest lies you can ever believe in ministry. To add to this, all good leaders have an insatiable appetite to keep growing and see success in what they are pouring into.

There's nothing in scripture or in history that suggests the early church planters "made it" and somehow graduated out of hardship when their churches got a certain size or their ministries became successful. The "make-it" myth is simply an import from the American business world. It's from the stories you read about in Forbes magazine of the young hotshot execs who started a company in their garage and sold it to Apple before the age of 35. It's from the ESPN articles about athletes who went under the radar for close to a decade before they were "discovered" and signed a multi-million dollar contract as a MLB team's starting ace.

If we're truly putting our hands on the plow and taking up the hard work of building a church and the kingdom of God, we never graduate from the tensions, challenges, hardships, and pains of doing full-time ministry. It doesn't get easier. In fact, it gets harder. Again, the truly ambitious pastor has an appetite that is insatiable. There are no amounts of success in the church that ever really satisfy a man or woman after God's heart, but if you're living close to the heart of God and depending on His Spirit, He makes you stronger. Your tolerance for pain gets higher, and your God gets much bigger. On this earth, if you ever buy into the lie that you've "made it", you're in a danger zone of complacency, denial, and apathy. You or I won't "make it" until every tribe, tongue, nation, and language on earth has heard the Gospel of Jesus Christ and as of right now, 68% of the world does not know Him or recognize Him as the rightful king of this earth.

Let that soak in for a second.

68% of the world's 7 billion is 4.7 billion people. One billion is a big number. A billion seconds is 31 years. A billion minutes ago was just after the time of Christ. Now imagine 4.7 billion. That's an *astronomical* number. 4.7 billion is a larger number of people that any of us can ever begin to wrap our minds around.

That's how many people on this earth don't know Christ. That's how many people on the earth will someday spend an eternity separated from Him unless something, somehow changes. How on earth can any pastor buy into the delusion and the satanic lie that his work is somehow done and that the intensity of his calling can be diminished just because his church has reached 1,000 people? For the record, 1,000 is 0.00002% of 4.7 billion, or a tiny drop in a vast ocean.

Even as I write these words, it feels so overwhelming to think about. Never have the words of Jesus in Matthew 9:37 seemed more applicable than this day and age. Listen to what Jesus says,

"Then he said to his disciples, "The harvest is plentiful, but the laborers are few; therefore pray earnestly to the Lord of the harvest to send out laborers into his harvest."

Notice how after Jesus points out that fact that there is a lot of work to be done, He commands the disciples to *pray earnestly?* He points out an issue and a problem, and then calls them to action! And the action has little to do with them pursuing their own kingdom via their own efforts, strategies or strength, but rather seeking His face, power, and presence in raising up and sending out laborers to bring in the harvest.

There is still a lot of work to be done. The laborers are few, and the harvest is plentiful. No church has "made it" as long as there are people around the world that have not fully surrendered their lives to Christ.

Authentic Pursuit: Building a Church from Nothing

As you reach a certain size and achieve certain milestones, there is a temptation to believe the lie that things will get a lot easier and the intensity that got you there in the first place can be done away with.

In the first few months of the 6th year of the Experience Community, we were able to catch our breaths for just a few moments before another wave of craziness started up again. We ended year five running strong at around 900 between all three services. We had a brand new staff, and had just hired an office manager to help us get better at organization. The year began for us with a staff leadership retreat, where we walked through the calendar of the year and talked about/coordinated all major events. It was a beautiful time of reflecting on the victories of the past year and looking ahead to what we were believing God for in the upcoming year. One of the coolest moments of that retreat was on a Friday night when we sat around with guitars and worshipped together as a staff. It just felt like we were all in the same place- grateful to God for what He had done, but expectant and a little scared at the same time for what was coming next. We didn't really know what we were getting into.

When we came back from the retreat and got back to reality, we experienced another growth surge that sent us over the 1,000 mark for the first time. While this was exciting and definitely something to celebrate and recognize, we choose to see it as a milestone- a point of remembrance in an important journey, but definitely not a destination. We celebrated and praised

Authentic Pursuit: Building a Church from Nothing

God for it, but we had to remember the importance of keeping our eyes fixed on what was ahead. Throughout the first part of that year, it seemed as a staff like all hell was coming against us.

For one thing, Josh and one of our elders who helps oversee our finances had been working with a church consulting firm to get our financial systems set up and a little more in order as we grew. Although it initially seemed like a good idea for us to go outside of the organization to get some help in establishing procedures, systems, and processes, it quickly dawned on us that it wasn't going to work. So many of the things this particular consulting firm wanted for us to do went against the vision and values that we had held to since we first began as a church (things like staying out of debt and staying conservative with our budgeting philosophies). Yet, we knew we were a growing church and needed to get more organized/professional. A very real tension suddenly rose up in us as an organization. Would we stay true to the things that we had always valued and what had made who we were, or would we change the ways we did things for the sake of being more professional and compromise our culture?

After several very intense months of battling this tension, we ultimately decided to part ways with the accounting company that really wanted to be our consultants. It was painful, but it affirmed in us the things in our church's vision that we weren't going to change. There were some lines in the sand we just weren't going to cross. We could grow, mature, and get more professional without losing our integrity. I remember this group would always tell us, "This is how other churches do things." Trying to get us to conform to their ways versus ours. *At the risk of sounding arrogant, we did not grow at this rate by doing things the way other churches had.*

The other challenge was space. We had 6 full time staff members (along with 3 part timers) but no office space. We had met with our landlord and were in the process of building out a space across the hallway for offices and classrooms, but for whatever reason the build out was moving at a glacial pace. During the week we would move tables around in the children's classrooms to create makeshift offices, but that got old very quickly. We also didn't have a reception area, so people would walk right in to our "offices" during important meetings or prayer times, making it very difficult to get work done or meet with people in private. Over time, this tension grew and it became increasingly difficult as a staff to stay connected and on task with our weekly goals. As the church grew and our space diminished, we took an "every man for himself" approach at finding a quiet place to work. At times it felt like an elaborate game of hide and seek. I still remember trying to sneak into the cry room in the nursery during the middle of the week (thinking it would be empty), only to open the door and find Kyle hiding out in there already with his makeshift office set up! The lack of space and lack of staff communication started taking its toll on us as a staff.

On top of all of the office chaos, life and all its struggles and sufferings still raged on. Two young families in our church received the diagnosis of cancer on their children; one a 2-year-old little girl, the other an 11-year-old boy. A woman named Heather, who had been homeless and we had been working with for the past year to get off the streets and get her life together, had also received a fatal diagnosis from her doctor. Still more people in our church came to us with reports of broken marriages and family members with illnesses and suffering in so many lives.

We had people around the clock praying and declaring healing over these precious lives. Our staff, pastors, and leadership team laid hands on each person, asking the Lord to do a miracle and believing in faith that it would come, but that spring, Heather went home to be with the Lord, as did our 11-year-old friend. There are some things that no matter how much we try to understand, we just can't. We know that God is Jehovah-Rapha, the God who declares Himself in Exodus 15:26 as the "the Lord who heals." We also know that God is completely in control and ultimately knows what is best for all of His children. As difficult as it was to do the funerals for two lives that seemed to end all too soon, we knew that God was still faithful and in complete control over all of it. And He is good. All the time.

We knew it in our heads, but as we came out of the crazy season in the first part of year 6, many of us struggled to accept it in our hearts. The offices were finally done and we moved in, trying to keep everything going while moving and preparing for a Sunday. On Easter Sunday, we had over 1,400 people between all three services. It was incredible, crazy, and supernatural. In spite of all our hardships and struggles, God was still moving, but as a staff, we had hit a bump in the road.

We were all discouraged and tired. The "every man for himself" mentality had seemed to work alright when we weren't sharing offices, but all of the sudden we found ourselves in the same space together with no idea how to work together. Things weren't getting done, time was being wasted, and communication was awful. *So in April of that year, we had to start learning how to be a staff. It was painful. We hurt and misunderstood each other, but we pushed through and worked towards coming together as a team.* Something we started doing then that we still keep doing is reading books together on leadership/church development and talking about them over lunch at the end of the week. This has kept all of us on the same page and it's been incredibly helpful to have outside voices speak to the tensions that we encounter every day as a staff.

Looking back, what we were going through as a staff was a normal part of team formation. *Any business leader will tell you that forming a high-functioning team takes time, and team members almost always go through easily recognizable stages as they go from being nearly strangers to a close knit family with common values, goals, and passions.* Psychologist Bruce Tuckman first came up with the memorable phrase "forming, storming, norming, and performing" in his 1965 article, "Developmental Sequence in Small Groups."[v] He used it to describe the path that most teams follow on their way to high performance.

In the "forming" stage, most team members are positive and polite. Some are anxious, as they haven't fully understood what work the team will do. Others are simply excited about the task ahead. As leader, you play a dominant role at this stage, because team members' roles and responsibilities aren't clear. This stage can last for some time, as people start to work together, and as they make an effort to get to know their new colleagues. At the end of year five and the very beginning of year six, we were definitely in the honeymoon "forming" stage. Everybody was excited to be working together, but no-one really knew what kind of team work we would have to pull together and eventually do.

In the "storming" stage, people start to push against the boundaries established in the forming stage. This is the stage where many teams fail. Storming often starts where there is a conflict between team members' natural working styles. People may work in different ways for all sorts of reasons, but if differing working styles cause unforeseen problems, they may become frustrated. Storming can also happen in other situations. For example, team members may challenge your authority, or jockey for position as their roles are clarified. Or, if you haven't defined clearly how the team will work, people may feel overwhelmed by their workload, or they could be uncomfortable with the approach you're using. Some may question the worth of the team's goal, and they may resist taking on tasks. Team members who stick with the task at hand may experience stress, particularly as they don't have the support of established processes, or strong relationships with their colleagues. When we first moved into our new offices, we were hurled headlong into the storming phase as we encountered conflict with learning how to work with each other and clarify our roles as a team.

Gradually, the team moves into the norming stage. This is when people start to resolve their differences, appreciate colleagues' strengths, and respect your authority as a leader. Now that your team members know one-another better, they may socialize together, and they are able to ask each other for help and provide constructive feedback. People develop a stronger commitment to the team goal, and you start to see good progress towards it. There is often a prolonged overlap between storming and norming, because, as new tasks come up, the team may lapse back into behavior from the storming stage.

The team reaches the performing stage when hard work leads, without friction, to the achievement of the team's goal. The structures and processes that you have set up support this well. As a leader, you can delegate much of your work, and you can concentrate on developing team members. It feels easy to be part of the team at this stage, and people who join or leave won't disrupt performance.[v]

Slowly, by God's unbelievable grace, He began building us up as a team. We learned how to appreciate each other's strengths, communicate to each other in a way we could understand, and respect each other and the positions that God had placed all of us in. *I truly believe that a lot of church staffs don't get to the "performing" phase because they haven't been willing to push through the unpleasant realities of "storming".* It take a lot of Holy Spirit given forgiveness, grace, humility and a high tolerance for pain to be able to go through necessary conflicts and storms with people you love and come out on the other side to talk about it, but it's the only way to create a high functioning team that works well together to labor for the Gospel.

By that summer, as a staff we were settling into our roles ("norming") and as a church we were running around 1,100. The children's ministry put on an amazing vacation bible school, the youth group did a weeklong local missions outreach called "Widows and Orphans", and we did a series on Proverbs and Song of Solomon. Some church growth experts say that your church isn't supposed to grow during the summer, but that summer, God moved and began stirring people's hearts, and in August we had a baptism service where we baptized over 74 people. We were also running near 1,200 on a pretty consistent basis.

Authentic Pursuit: Building a Church from Nothing

With that many people attending on a weekend, it became impossible for me as a senior pastor to establish and maintain personal relationships with everyone at our church. Although I love meeting new people and try as much as I can to build relationships with as many people in our church as possible, we grew to a point that summer where I simply could not connect with everyone on a personal level.

This became a new challenge for me as a teacher. In the past, I was communicating to people I knew personally and had done life with. But now I had to get to a point where I could communicate what God had put on my heart in a way that moved them, even the people I didn't know personally. I had to work at becoming articulate, practical, and as Biblical as possible. *I seek to end every single lesson with an invitation to know and experience God personally. This became something I placed a lot of emphasis on the bigger we got, as I don't know the kind of struggles that the people sitting in our seats on a Sunday may be going through. It's important that I show them Jesus and give them a chance to respond.*

With that many people attending on a weekend, the amount of criticism you receive will increase. Some of it will come from people who might have valid concerns but not a lot of tact or graciousness, some of it will come from those who are wounded and criticize you out of hurt or fear, and some will come from those who are just flat out critical and hateful. Regardless of the reasons why, criticism never feels great and can be difficult to take, especially from people that love and trust. Something that we learned as a staff was to go directly to the source of the criticism and use the phrase, "help me understand _____" as a means to hear someone out when they have a criticism against anything going on in our church. It's gone such a long way in helping get things out in the open and letting people know that we care about what they think, but we will never tolerate gossip. *I will also say that over time, if you are teaching your congregation the Bible with love and humility, you will not receive overwhelming amounts of criticism. But, if you do, you can put the pressure on His Word and not yourself.*

As we moved into the fall, we dove headlong into the gospel of Matthew and kept moving forward in growing as a church. A new phenomenon we kept experiencing were sales calls from church growth consultants and companies that had reportedly caught wind of our growth and now wanted our business. It always seemed like they offered to help us find the new latest gimmick or trick that would "take us over the edge" and get us that ever coveted mega-church status (as if that's what we were truly after). Over time, it just started making us sick. I wrestled with the thought that we had sold out the vision that God had given me six years earlier when I started the church. How did we get from a small gathering of misfits, weirdos, and hippies to a church of 1,200 that was now garnering the attention of church marketing companies? It kept me up at night, not because I thought the "success" was a bad thing, but it bothered me what our American church culture views as "success" and what we seem to do with those we view as successful.

So one night as I was praying about all of the tension, weirdness and pressure we were feeling to become more "churchy", I heard God speak to me very clearly. I decided that night that I was going to do something radical and obey Him. I was going to do something out of the ordinary, bold, and definitely not "churchy" (at least what I had known to be "churchy"). I heard from God that night that I was to look at what we had in our bank account, take 20% of our money, and give it away to other churches that needed it more than we did. I got online and looked up how evangelical churches in the Northeast were doing. According to my research, Burlington, Vermont; Boston, Massachusetts; and Providence, Rhode Island were ranked near the top of the most "post-Christian" cities in America[v]. A "mega-church" up there was one that ran around 100-200 people. I couldn't buy into the lie that somehow we had achieved "success" and had "made it" when our brothers and sisters in the northeast were still laboring to make disciples in a difficult mission field.

So the next morning at church, I got up and announced that we were going to give away roughly $40,000. I told our congregation that the point of church was not to build ourselves a bigger kingdom here so we could get more and more comfortable and spiritually obese, but the point of us giving, serving, and assembling was so that we could go out and make more disciples of Christ in dark places where Christ isn't known. People applauded, but I think some thought I was absolutely crazy. Regardless, that Sunday there was a check in the offering for $50,000. Someone had heard from the Lord before I said anything that they were supposed to give it all away.

That fall, I traveled to Burlington, Vermont; Salem, Massachusetts; and Providence, Rhode Island to meet with pastors in churches that were working to make the gospel known. I handed each of them a check for a portion of what God told me to give away. What we have done since then is to pick a new church in the Northeast every year and add them to the list of churches we already support up there. Maybe that sounds ridiculous and irresponsible to someone growing a business or a secular organization, but I would rather listen to God and His heart for how we are to grow as a church that makes Jesus known all across the world. A win is not just butts in the seats on a Sunday. A win is changed lives and disciples made in every continent across the face of this earth. We never want to get so "churchy" and tame that we can't be radical for the Gospel of Jesus, and as we grow, sadly, that becomes increasingly more difficult.

In year 6, we learned that keeping our hearts and our values centered on God becomes increasingly harder as the world's view of success is achieved, but we also learned that our only hope is found in tying ourselves to the mast of His Gospel, His grace, and His commission to make much of His glory. Church growth and societal trends will come and go, but He is the same yesterday, today, and forever. We're not in this for our fame, we're in it for His. Growing with integrity is painful. Keeping our hearts pure in the face of temptation, tension, and trials hurts, but Jesus said, "Blessed are the pure in heart, for they will see God." (Matthew 5:8). I'll take seeing God any day over seeing our names on a magazine or billboard.

WHAT WE LEARNED-

Don't Stop with Your Intensity

In communities all across the US and world, there are plenty of churches that at one time were growing, vibrant, and healthy, but are now, for the most part, irrelevant. Worse than that, many churches that were at one time power hitters for the kingdom of God are now nonexistent. In a 2013 sermon, Pastor James McDonald revealed some shocking realities about the state of the American church. He said,

"Of the 250,000 Protestant churches in America, 200,000 are either stagnant (with no growth) or declining. That is 80% of the churches in America and maybe the one you attend, if you attend at all. 4,000 churches close their doors every single year. There is less than half of the number of churches today than there were only 100 years ago. 3,500 people leave the church every single day. Since 1950, there are one third fewer churches in the U.S."[v]

The fact that 4,000 churches in the U.S. close their doors every single year should be a sobering reminder to every pastor and church planter that no matter how "successful" they may seem or how many milestones they may have achieved, no church is exempt from losing a grip on what made them great and fading into death or irrelevancy. Every church is vulnerable to decline and a fall, but if their leaders understand the factors that contribute to a fall, they can stumble and still recover. One of the great temptations that I believe can lead to a decline in a church is lessening the intensity once certain milestones are reached. For churches, usually those milestones are attendance or buildings.

It's a common understanding in the world of sports that success is elusive to any team that plays not to lose instead of playing to win. When churches forget that the win is not simply keeping the lights turned on in a nice facility, or the giving adequate enough to meet the budgets, or the attendance at an reasonable level, this can lead to a lack of intensity in the way that decisions are made as a church.

Churches can end up misaligning their priorities to simply "maintain" their initial success instead of keeping their vision fixed upon whatever is next. We learned that focused intensity must always be modeled by the senior leaders of the church. If the senior pastor and elders are content with mediocrity, the church will almost always be content with mediocrity, but if the senior leaders are *intense* in their pursuit of revival and Gospel multiplication (and that manifests in their prayer life, personal evangelism, discipleship, ministry work ethic, and commitment to *ACTION, not just talk)*, the church will catch that same vision and intensity.

Building a Team Takes Work

How many times in the world of sports do we see teams loaded with talent, potential, and star appeal that somehow can't get it together and pull off a win? It happens all the time. In the off-season, loads of money is spent as the big names are drafted or picked up as free-agents and all of the fans take to social media to prognosticate about how great their beloved team will be in the upcoming season. But year after year, there are teams loaded with potential that *should* be good, but just aren't. Why?

Because you can't purchase teamwork, you can't buy character, and you certainly can't fabricate synergy or unity amongst people that don't share a common vision for how they will achieve the goal they all want. In the church world, it's really not that different. So many churches will go after the heavy-hitters from their respective denominations that are loaded with talent, grade-A ministry pedigrees, and a lot of success under their belts, believing somehow that this star player on their team will finally ensure them success. Yet, many of

Authentic Pursuit: Building a Church from Nothing

those same churches get frustrated when those individuals display a misalignment of vision, character issues, an ego, and an inability to work well with others.

There must be an intentional effort put forth by the senior leaders to grow a staff into an effective, high-functioning, synergistic team. It's not as simple as handing everyone their job descriptions when they're hired, meeting once a week for staff meeting for a check-in, and then retreating to your respective offices until Sundays. It takes work. It takes time to get to know each other's personalities, strengths, weaknesses, sensitivities, motivating factors, core values, love languages, personal histories, and spiritual gifts. When *trust* is built amongst a staff, and everyone knows that the vision of the church is more important than their own individual egos and personal ambitions- there's no limit as to what can be accomplished.

For the sake of practicality, here are some thing we've done and still do to build our team on a regular basis.

Staff prayer

Every week, we meet together on Monday mornings before staff meeting to pray for each other and to pray for our church. We make this a priority- just as important as staff meetings and just as crucial. We make a point to get vulnerable with each other, sharing any needs we have in our ministries and our personal lives.

195

Authentic Pursuit: Building a Church from Nothing

Leadership Teaching
At the start of a staff meeting, Corey usually brings a passage of scripture, a short article or a devotional about leadership and shares it with the staff. We talk about it and how it applies to us in our ministries, as we reflect on the past week and prepare for any upcoming responsibilities.

Leadership Books
Every week, we read a chapter of a book together and then we meet together at the end of the week to discuss it. Having outside voices speak to the challenges of day-to-day ministry in our context has been incredibly helpful.

Staff Retreats
Every year, as a staff we get away and go on a leadership retreat (where we bring in other pastors and leaders to pour into and encourage us as a staff/leaders) and planning retreat (where we go over the yearly calendar and share our vision for the year). These times have been incredibly helpful and encouraging to get re-charge and a fresh vision from God.

Staff Lunch
At the end of each week we go to lunch together. I know this doesn't seem like a ground-breaking, revolutionary idea, but it builds us up as a team and a staff to spend time out together just enjoying each other's company.

Authentic Pursuit: Building a Church from Nothing

When we get lunch together, there are no agendas, no talk about ministry or leadership- just lunch. There was a noticeable difference in how we got along on Sundays and throughout the week when we made the investment into each other as friends through sharing a meal together.

Open Channels of Communication
Something we strive for in all of our meetings and communication is for it be open and honest, with no tensions or conflicts that are unresolved between leaders and departments. We tell each other the truth in love, and have the tough conversations for the sake of unity (even if a lot of those conversations happen behind closed doors). Our vision is too important to have a divided team.

Avoid Other's Assumptions about Who You're Supposed to Be

When the calls started coming in from church consulting firms and vendors seeking our business on things like video announcements, church mailers, or A/V equipment, we always seemed to hear a lot of name-dropping. Companies, consultants and vendors would almost always mention the mega-churches in our region that employed their services. Now from a business sense, I get that. You're wanting to build credibility by mentioning the clients that use your services so we know that you're not selling snake-oil. But when people coming to your church (or even in positions of leadership) assume that you're going to start a program or build onto your facilities or hire a certain staff position *simply because it's what the mega-churches are doing-* watch out. You are called by God to follow His vision for your church, not mimic or parrot the vision of some church down the street. Hear me out, there's nothing wrong with employing a ministry strategy or tool from another church if it fits within your vision and it's working for them. My point is, don't change your vision for your church or make significant changes to your culture simply because it's what _____ (*insert mega-church name*) is doing. You're not _____. Be what God has asked you to be.

Be Radical

If you're reading this book as a pastor or church-planter and haven't heard anything helpful thus far, please get this- YOU ARE NOT CALLED BY GOD TO BE A PROFESSIONAL. Listen to the words of our true pastor, that one that planted this whole movement we call the church-

"But Jesus called them to him and said, "You know that the rulers of the Gentiles lord it over them, and their great ones exercise authority over them. *It shall not be so among you.* But whoever would be great among you must be your servant, and whoever would be first among you must be your slave, even as the Son of Man came not to be served but to serve, and to give his life as a ransom for many." (Matthew 20:25-28)

Do you get that? This is coming from a homeless, Jewish carpenter/Rabbi who in a few chapters will get on his hands and knees and scrub the dirty feet of blue-collar fishermen. This is coming from the one who cared more about the plan of redemption for humanity than He did about His own personal comfort. This is spoken by the one who willingly gave up His throne to take on human flesh to be beaten, mocked, and spit upon so that the Father's will could be accomplished.

That's not professional. This kind of barbaric and radical sacrifice and obedience is a far cry from the world of pastors who make six figures, drive luxury cars, and spend more time gerrymandering with the affluent than they do washing the feet of the poor and destitute.

Pastor- don't you *ever* buy into the blasphemous, heretical nonsense that your "success" can buy you out of being radical in your obedience and sacrifice. When you said "yes" to following Jesus as a pastor and leader of God's people, you were saying yes to a cross, not your own parking space. Jesus was not a tame, cultured, and cavalier professional. That leads me to believe that you are not to be a "professional" either. This is a calling for wild-men, not for "professionals".

WORKS CITED-

Tuckman, B. (n.d.). Developmental Sequence in Small Groups. Psychological Bulletin, 384-399.

http://www.mindtools.com/pages/article/newLDR_86.htm

http://cities.barna.org/the-most-post-christian-cities-in-america/

James McDonald, Walk in the Word Ministries

CHAPTER 9

MOVING INTO DEEPER AND MORE UNCOMFORTABLE WATER

"Those who know Your name trust in You because You have not abandoned those who seek You, Yahweh." (Psalm 9:10)

Authentic Pursuit: Building a Church from Nothing

Year 7 of our journey thus far has been unbelievable, exciting, and exhausting all at the same time. It seems like this has always been how God has operated in our midst, so I'm not at all surprised that this year is any different. It's so crazy, at the beginning of the year our staff wrote down what they expected God to do this year in our church, and one of these I wrote was 30% growth in 2015. As I am typing this, it is May, and we have already grown 35% this year. The only thing we can do at this point in the journey is to keep pursuing Him for what's next while simultaneously holding onto the vision He gave us at the very beginning. Some of the newer challenges/opportunities we've faced this year have been-

Saturday services.

Near the end of last year, we were faced with the reality that we were already running out of space in our new building that we had spent so much time, energy, and prayer to get into. To make matters more complicated, we were only running out of space in our two morning services (9 & 11 AM on Sundays). Our 6 P.M. services were anemic. As much as we tried to get volunteers to staff our children's ministries for the 6 P.M., the volunteers just weren't coming. It's difficult for people with families and full-time jobs to come out to serve late on a school-night. Without childcare, most young families can't come out to an evening service. So we were experiencing lopsided growth and a definite barrier to growing any further. We were in a bind and we knew something had to change.

After a lot of thought, prayer, and conversation, we made the decision to move the 6 P.M. Sunday service to Saturday nights (at 5 P.M.) and add an additional service on Saturdays at 7 P.M. That way, volunteers could serve at the 5 P.M. and worship at the 7 P.M., or worship at the 5 and serve at the 7. When one plants a growing church, it is important to consider "pairing" services together. This gives people the opportunity to serve and attend service. Not only that, but families with children can come out on Saturday nights and not have to get up early the next morning to take the kids the school. So far, our Saturday services have been an incredible success. We've experienced another growth surge since the switch of almost 350 people in just 4 months, and our staff has been enjoying Sunday nights off for the first time ever. It's amazing what a little bit of tweaking can do. We went from 1150 people in December 2014 to a quick jump to 1600 people by April 2015. God keeps doing amazing things, and we try to keep up.

Facility Expansion.

As much as the Saturday services have been a huge help in managing our growth this year, we know that they're only a short-term solution. In the children's/nursery area, we're running out of room in the Sunday morning services especially. We're also experiencing growth pains in the area of small groups and meeting spaces for volunteer teams, but God knows all of our needs before we ask or even know about them ourselves, and in His sovereignty has made available around 45,000 sq. feet of unfinished warehouse space in the building we already have. We'll start working soon to turn that into a new sanctuary, classrooms for children's/nursery, a fellowship hall, offices, a prayer chapel, and life group rooms.

Renewed emphasis on prayer.

As our church has grown larger, the obstacles we face seem more complicated and the solutions less obvious. Now more-so than *ever* we need the hand of God, the provision of God, and the presence of God on us as a church and us as leaders especially. Recently, the Lord has been kind enough to reveal to us that prayer was desperately lacking in our church. A few months ago, as a staff we picked up the book *The Prayer Saturated Church* by Cheryl Sacks and started reading it together. These words from the first chapter seemed to leap with conviction and power right off of the page - "When I think of the church in other nations around the world, words come to mind such as all-night prayer meetings, prayer and fasting chains, and multi-church and community-wide prayer and worship gatherings. What is the American church known for? I think people might say we're known for great programs, effective small groups, excellent resources, or good administration. Most people probably wouldn't think of the American church as being known for dynamic prayer."

Jesus made in clear in Mark 11:17, "My house will be called a house of prayer for all nations." If we were honest with ourselves, our church wasn't truly being known as a house of prayer. Prayer happened in our church before services, during services, and even in special prayer meetings, but the predominant practice of our church wasn't prayer. This drove us as a staff and leadership to a place of repentance and the pursuit of truly making our church a place where all activity comes from a place of communion and fellowship with God. We want all of our strategies, plans, and power to accomplish the mission and vision God has given us to come out of a place of prayer. If we're not doing that, we have no reason to believe that we're even remotely close to being called a "house of prayer", and by default, we can't expect God to bless something that isn't what He wants or intends. We're far from where we want to be, but we've recently starting opening up our prayer room in the mornings from 6:30-9:30, launched two new prayer groups, and plan on teaching a series this summer on prayer. We've seen radical and awesome things come out of a renewed emphasis on prayer, and what's incredible is that we've just started and have so far to go.

There are a lot of books, podcasts, videos, and teachings out there about churches, church ministry, pastoral work, and even church planting. There are endless numbers of theories, strategies, ideas, and paradigms for how to do this thing called church, many of which complement and contradict the others simultaneously. It would be naïve to assume that we at the Experience Community in our limited training and experience can somehow add anything new to the scholastic body of work in this area. In other words, we don't know a lot about anything. If you met any of us and spent some time getting to know us, you'd agree wholeheartedly. We're not very "churchy". We're not especially eloquent. None of us are "qualified" to be "professionals" at this thing called church, but when I sit back and think about it, maybe that's why God picked us.

Paul wrote in 1 Corinthians 1:27, "God has chosen what is foolish in the world to shame the wise, and God has chosen what is weak in the world to shame the strong." If anyone fits this description, it's us. We are the fools and we are the weak. We were once the cocaine, pill, and porn addicts, the alcoholics, the homeless, the suicidal, the unfaithful, the rebellious, and the depressed. We had nothing going for us in the eyes of this world, but God chose us- and in that choosing of us redeemed, restored, and renewed us through His spirit so that we never could point to our academic accolades or our denominational pedigrees as reasons for our success. There is only one simple explanation for why this whole crazy thing has worked thus far- God. There is absolutely no reason any of us on staff and leadership should be doing what we're doing. God has been so gracious and so good to us in ways that make absolutely no sense.

There aren't any ground breaking new strategies I want to leave you with, just a few challenges and closing thoughts on what it means to radically pursue God's plan in pastoral ministry, and starting a church from nothing.

We are not "professionals"

I'm fully convinced that the job of a pastor or a church-planter is not one that should be looked upon or viewed as "professional". It's not a profession or a job. It's a lifestyle, and if you're not prepared to give your life, don't sign up. People come to me all the time asking what the "secret sauce" to our success is. They want to hear about quick fixes and magic bullets and secret paradigms that will launch their congregation into the realms of mega-church-dom. But they don't want to hear about me not taking a salary for the first 2 years of leading the church. They don't want to hear about me scrubbing toilets in a factory or working the night shift at a gym while I wrote my messages. *In other words, many people want success without sacrifice.*

The story is told of a world famous violinist that once had a woman approach him after one of his concerts. She said to him, "I'd give my life to play as beautifully as you do." To which he replied, "I did." This calling to build and strengthen the Church of God is not one that should be undertaken by those who simply want a "full-time job" in church ministry because of some idyllic fantasies of what being a pastor actually looks like. It's not a job that can be confined to typical office hours or a "normal" workload. It's not a job for tame, white-collar "professionals". It's a calling that requires barbarous tenacity and faith and a willingness to *do whatever it takes* to see God's kingdom grow.

Not only that, but it's a calling that requires us to *never* grow more reliant on our training, experience, or expertise in the field of church ministry than on the power of God to constantly fill us and sustain us in the work that He's given us to do. In his book *Brothers, We Are Not Professionals*[v], John Piper offers this prayer for pastors around the world-

"Banish professionalism from our midst, Oh God, and in its place put passionate prayer, poverty of spirit, hunger for God, rigorous study of holy things, white-hot devotion to Jesus Christ, utter indifference to all material gain, and unremitting labor to rescue the perishing, perfect the saints, and glorify our sovereign Lord.

Humble us, O God, under your mighty hand, and let us rise, not as professionals, but as witnesses and partakers of the sufferings of Christ."

A High Tolerance for Pain

I once heard Pastor Craig Groeschel give a message to pastors where he said something remarkable. He said, "Sometimes the difference between where you are and where God wants you to be is the pain that you are unwilling to endure ... In fact, I will argue all day long that your potential in every area of your life is equal to the pain you are willing to endure." This strikes a chord with those of us involved in pastoral ministry and church planting on any level because of just how painful and difficult this calling tends to be. From engaging in necessary but difficult confrontations that could lead to potential church splits and top donors leaving, to fighting for your vision, to getting betrayed by those who you thought had your back- this whole endeavor requires unbelievable diligence, endurance, perseverance, and yes, a high tolerance for pain. There will be times when you seriously consider quitting. It's not a question of "if", it's a question of "when". And *when* you do consider quitting, go back to that time when you were certain that you first heard from God that this was what you were to spend your life doing. If you never had that moment, maybe it's time to hit your knees and ask for one. You will be hurt. You will be criticized. You will suffer. It won't be easy, but that's never a good reason not to obey what God is asking of you. Jesus never promised easy, He only said it'd be worth it.

Blessed Are the Pure in Heart

I'm going to say this as frankly as I know how- if you want to make money, get famous, or gain influence- go sell insurance, move to Hollywood or run for local office. Even if you're doing all of the right things in church planting or pastoral ministry for all of the wrong reasons, your works can go completely unrewarded and unnoticed by God. This was Jesus's indictment against the Pharisees. They did *all* of the right things- they prayed, gave to the poor, tithed, and were faithful in teaching in the synagogues. But they did it for themselves. They did it so people would notice them and they'd get accolades and applause. And Jesus says, "Truly I tell you, they have received their reward in full." (Matthew 6:2) In other words, they won't be receiving *anything* from God for their "religious devotion". Their ultimate and final reward is simply empty flattery and praise from *people*. People that don't even really know the true condition of their hearts. Even if we have everyone around us fooled, God sees our intentions and our motives. And if our hearts aren't pure in building His church for the right reasons, we cannot expect to experience His rewards and His presence. Jesus said, "Blessed are the *pure in heart, for they shall see God.*" (Matt. 5:8).

Do you really want to see God in your ministry? Do you want to see Him move in your church and move in your community and flip everything upside down in the way that only He can do? Jesus said that this can only happen when our hearts are pure. This happens when we *truly* desire for His name to be exalted, not our own. This happens when we embrace obscurity and lower ourselves in humility, taking on the mind of Christ as a servant who washed feet- not as a rock star pastor with 2 million followers on Twitter and their own parking spot.

Barbaric, tenacious faith.

One of the definitions for the word "barbaric" is primitive or unsophisticated. I think we all could use a little barbarism in our faith. In other words, I think we need to get to a point where we're willing to look a little undignified, silly, and "unintelligent" in the eyes of the people around of us in order to simply and unsophisticatedly obey and live out the calling and commands of God on our lives. I'm convinced that if every believer (and every pastor especially) simply got over their pride and said "yes" to whatever God told them, our world and our churches would look drastically different. Sure, people will misunderstand and criticize you, maybe even your family and close friends. But what does that matter? What does that cost you? Your pride? That should have been nailed to the cross a long time ago.

We need to get it into our thick skulls that the only thing we really have to offer God is a willingness to be used by Him. When we give our everything for His purposes, without holding or taking anything back, He can do amazing things with the most broken and unqualified people, but there must first be a willingness to step out in faith and obedience, and a determination to continue trusting and following Him, even when it seems illogical.

Key Values and Character

If you're thinking/praying about planting a church, I want to encourage you early on to sit down with a pen and a piece of paper and write down the key values and character qualities that you feel are essential and non-negotiable for you and everyone else involved in your ministry to strive for and display in everything you do. Let these things be the ballasts that keep you steady and the foundations that you build everything on. It's so important to clarify not just "what" you want to build, but "how" you want to go about it. If you don't take the time to make that clear to everyone involved, don't be surprised if your vision gets hijacked. Here are a few of our core values that you're more than welcome to plagiarize.

Clarity

Matthew 28:19-20 says this, "Go therefore and make disciples of all nations, baptizing them in the name of the Father and of the Son and of the Holy Spirit, teaching them to observe all that I have commanded you..." Jesus was very clear with His disciples about *what* He wanted and about what they were to do- (1) make disciples, (2) baptize them, and (3) teach them to observe His commandments. It seems very simple, but unfortunately in the American church we can get so caught up in pursuits that seem to be about everything

BUT the Great Commission. So for us, a key value is clarity.

Clarity is the art of knowing what's actually going on in your church and ministry. We want clarity in knowing what each ministry/program/outreach is actually *doing,* and we want to have freedom to say no to it/pull the plug on it if it's not in alignment with our vision. We want clarity in understanding where each ministry fits in the process of discipleship in our church and what that ministry is doing to help lead people to Christ. We want clarity in knowing if ministries are actually taking people somewhere, not simply filling up their time. So for every ministry/program/outreach in our church, we ask, "Where do we want our people to be? What do we want them to become? What needs do they need met? Will this ministry take them there? Is this ministry fulfilling the great commission?" We strive to provide clarity to our volunteers. We want to tell them what they're actually doing when they serve. For every volunteer on every team, we want to show what "a win" looks like in their particular ministry. For example, a "win" in hospitality is if someone gets connected to a Life Group. A "win" in Life Group is someone taking an active step to grow in their faith (be it baptism, serving, or giving). We also want to provide clarity to the people who give financially to the church. Each week we highlight a ministry that is only made possible through the financial support of donors, we show where every dollar in our budget goes (including salaries) twice a year in our vision services, and

I (Josh) send a letter to first time givers detailing some of our financial controls and procedures. We want to give clarity to everyone in our church about who we are, where we're going, who we want to be, and what we're going to do about it.

The monthly Next class helps us make these things exceptionally clear to new-comers, as do the vision services. Most importantly, we want to provide clarity to all of our staff. Every staff member has a written job description that we revisit often to make sure all of our expectations are clearly communicated- not just what we want them to do, but also what we may want them to *stop* doing. We also perform staff evaluations twice a year, so we have a clear idea of the job performance and wins for all of our staff members. We don't ever want to confuse simply "staying busy" for making progress. In short, we strive to make everything we do simple and clear to everyone around us.

Communication

Along with clarity comes communication. Communication is defined as the imparting or exchanging of information. Just as importantly as *knowing* what's going on in all of our ministries in our church, we want to be strategic about who, where, when, how, and what we communicate to our people. In a day and age where people are bombarded with stimulus and information on a moment-by-moment basis, a strategy for how you are going to get them *life-saving* information is imperative. Communication for us is more than just an obligatory announcement time at the beginning of a Sunday service. It's having a strategy for social media, utilizing videos for certain information, knowing when/how to use print media or handouts/fliers, using appropriate audio/visual aids during the teaching of the Word, and understanding what will actually catch people's eyes and capture their attention. Hear me out- I'm not suggesting becoming a glorified marketing company and resorting to gimmicks to get people in the doors of your church. That's tacky and will probably turn more people off than anything else (or attract people that will show up for all of the wrong reason. See Matt. 11:7-9). What I am saying is that if your church wants a seat at the table in our media-saturated/information-age marketplace of ideas, it would do you good to learn to speak the language of our culture. It is possible (and quite Biblical, I would argue, 1 Cor. 9:22) to speak the language of a culture without compromising to the values of a culture and watering down the message of the Gospel. We see ourselves as missionaries to our city. A good missionary goes to language school, learns the culture, and interacts with the people-all for the purpose of knowing how to communicate the Gospel to these people in a way they can understand. When a missionary does that overseas, we applaud them for their cultural awareness and love for the Gospel, but when a church does that in the states, we label them as emergent liberals. Maybe we need to gain a better and more

Biblical understanding of culture and the ways in which we are called to engage it.

Transparency and Authenticity

I've said it earlier and I'll say it again- if you met and spent any length of time with any of us, you wouldn't come away impressed with how much we know. We don't really know a lot, but here's what we've discovered- when we're honest about *who we are, and who we're not*, that's attractive to people. When we're honest as leaders about our struggles, our failures, our insecurities, our fears, our hurts, and our heartaches, it frees people up to see us simply as human beings in need of scandalous, life-transforming grace. True life change doesn't happen until people are honest about who they truly are, and people tend to not be honest about who they really are if no-one else is. People can sense fake. They can't be absolutely certain about it, but they can sense if someone is insincere. We've found that nothing stifles a culture of grace more than pretense.

When we give people permission to be honest about who they are, where they are, and what they are, without fear of rejection, we put the Gospel in action. The Gospel says, "Even on our *best days*, none of us deserve what we've been given through the cross." We so often gravitate towards pretense (or the appearance of being something we're not) because we don't truly believe that. We're afraid that if people really knew who we were, they wouldn't love us. The cross says that God sees and know us completely and still chose to die for us. And if that's the love that Jesus showed us, we are compelled to show that love to each other.

So what exactly does that look like? It's not unusual for Corey to share a personal story or a struggle he's been having in one of his messages. It's understood that all of our office doors are always open for people who need to come in and confess/get prayed for/talk about hurts or struggles with any of our staff without judgment. The same policy is understood around the office for us as a staff with each other. Transparency and community is something that has to be modeled first by the leaders. That shows the people in your church that it's safe to stop pretending and start being real. But we also stress the importance of holiness as well. Simply being authentic is not in and of itself beneficial to someone's spiritual growth. There must be a willingness to let God come in and change the parts of us that are broken. God always comes to us where we are, but He never leaves us how He finds us.

Humility

Humility is a tricky thing to write about. If one ever believes that they are *nailing it* at displaying this character quality, then by default, they aren't. So I want to be careful in proclaiming as a church our aptness and mastery of this elusive attribute.

I never want any of us to forget where we came from. I never want any of us to feel entitled to any of the things or success that God, through His grace and grace alone, has given us. I never want any of us to look down our noses at churches smaller than us, bigger than us, more traditional than us or more progressive than us, and feel that subversive sense of superiority creep into our hearts. I say this in the sincere hopes that this won't come across as false humility, but we don't deserve any of this. We're not smarter than anyone, more spiritual than anyone, more faithful than anyone, or more prayerful than anyone. We've made more mistakes in this journey than most.

I think it is *essential* to always be reminding ourselves of these truths. We want to always be about Jesus and nothing else. When we make Him the focus, and not ourselves, we are forced to contemplate the role that He told us to play as His disciples on earth. He said, "…whoever wants to become great among you must be your servant." (Matt. 20:26). Elsewhere in Scripture we're told,

"Have this mind among yourselves, which is your in Christ Jesus, who, though he was in the form of God, did not count equality with God a thing to be grasped, *but emptied himself*, by taking the form of a *servant*, being born in the likeness of men. And being found in human form, he *humbled himself by being obedient* to the point of death, even death on a cross." (Phil. 2:5-8)

We want to be emptied of ourselves. We want to take the form of servants, and we want to humble ourselves in obedience. I think humility is making a big deal about God and taking the focus off of ourselves.

We want people in our church to know and follow their one and only savior- Jesus. The moment it becomes about any of us, we're missing it entirely.

The Harvest is Abundant

"Then Jesus went to all the towns and villages, teaching in their synagogues, preaching the good news of the kingdom, and healing every disease and every sickness. When He saw the crowds, He felt compassion for them, because they were weary and worn out, like sheep without a shepherd. Then He said to His disciples, "The harvest is abundant, but the workers are few. Therefore, pray to the Lord of the harvest to send out workers into His harvest." **(Matthew 9:35-38, HCSB)**

A few summers ago, on a hot August afternoon, I (Josh) went out with my wife and mother-in-law to a blueberry farm to pick some blueberries (what else do you do at a blueberry farm?). It seemed a little silly to me, as we could just walk down the produce section at Publix and get blueberries, but I kept my mouth shut and tagged along. As we were getting our buckets from the landowner and getting instructions on how to pick the berries, something he said struck a chord with me.

He said, "Since the berries are ripe, you won't need to do a lot of picking. Just run your fingers down the vine, and the ripe ones will fall right into the bucket."

As we walked through the blueberry bushes that afternoon, God reminded me of the words of Jesus in Matthew 9. *The harvest is abundant, but the workers are few.* Every time a fistful of ripe, juicy berries dropped in the bucket as a result of me doing very little (simply running my hand across the vine), those words of Jesus echoed in my mind- *the harvest is abundant, but the workers are few*. I looked out at all of the blueberry bushes that were ripe for picking and were ready for somebody, for anybody, to simply run their hands down a vine, and wondered why so few people came out for the harvest. Sure, it was work. It was hot out there and there were thorns every now and again. But then again, it wasn't. All we did was run our hands down a vine, and the reward was far greater than the "sacrifice" we put in. There was something so satisfying about seeing your bucket get full of farm-fresh, ripe, all natural blueberries. Every time we ate blueberries for the next month or so, it meant something. I started feeling bad for the people who never had the pleasure of picking blueberries. They were missing out on something beautiful.

It's not a perfect metaphor, but I think ministry at times can be a bit like that. There are *crowds* of people in my city and yours that are weary and worn out, like sheep without a shepherd. They are ready to meet with Jesus. They are ripe for picking, but unfortunately, there are few people that want to grab a bucket, endure the heat, and engage them with love and truth so that they can simply fall into His arms. We'd rather the berries come to us on our terms.

1 Corinthians 3:7 says, "...neither the one who plants nor the one who waters is anything, but only God who gives the growth." It's God who saves. It's God who redeems, restores, renews, and gives new life to the

broken. But for whatever reason, He chooses to use imperfect people like us to run our hands down the vine and help with this harvest. We don't do much, but the job we've been given is the most important one in the universe. We have the choice to either join Him in obedience or miss out on something incredibly beautiful.

Our prayer and hope for the Church of Jesus around the world is that we get busy and get to work. The harvest is abundant and beautiful

WORKS CITED-

Piper, J. (2002). *Brothers, We Are Not Professionals: A Plea to Pastors for Radical Ministry*. B&H Books.

Sacks, C. (2004). *The prayer saturated church: A comprehensive handbook for prayer leaders*. Colorado Springs, CO: NavPress.

CHAPTER 10
SOME FAQ'S

Authentic Pursuit: Building a Church from Nothing

Over the years, we've gotten a lot questions on what we do and how we do what we do, so we thought we'd try to answer as many of them as we could in this chapter.

Our Church Distinctives

• We are a Bible-centered, Spirit led, Spirit filled, and non-denominational congregation.

• We are theologically conservative and methodologically progressive (We major on the major doctrines, while minoring on the minors. We create and engage culture as missionaries to our city and community.)

• We are a congregation that is on mission (We believe that every Christ Follower is called to ministry, so we strive to help every person discover, develop, and use their talents in ministry.)

• We hold a commitment to excellence in every area of ministry (We want to create intentional environments that eliminate distractions so that people can meet with God).

• We are a process driven church (not an event driven church). This can be summed up in our Mission & Vision Statement:

• We believe in the values of simplicity, structure & authenticity (All ministries and happenings in the church are heavily vetted through the vision statement & church process. If they don't align, we say no. Our Sunday services follow a very basic format with most of the time dedicated to worship and the teaching of the Word through expository, verse-by-verse teaching. If a ministry isn't effective or authentically engaging people according to our vision statement, we pull the plug.)

• We are staff led, elder guarded (The senior pastor is the leader of the church, because we believe that "follow me" works better than "follow we." However, we also believe in Spiritual accountability. We appoint Elders that serve in the church by holding the pastors spiritually accountable, offering counsel, communicating and vision-casting, and helping to co-ordinate ministry needs).

• We are committed to giving back and serving our community (20% as of now, but we hope one day to reach 50% of every dollar given to our church being given back to Murfreesboro through community service projects. 5,000, our homeless and low-income ministry, is a huge part of our culture as a church and feeds breakfast at a local park every Sunday morning to those in need).

• We believe in discipling and equipping people within our church for leadership needs rather than hiring outside "ministry professionals" (It's unusual for us to fill a staff position with someone who has not come up through the process & vision statement of our church. We find that it creates more unity and "buy-in" on our ministry teams when we're staffed and led by people who are committed to the vision and culture of our church, not just seeking a "career" in ministry).

Do you require membership?

We don't do membership per se at the church. We just decided that instead of doing what a lot of traditional churches do like signing up commitment pledges or cards, we would take a different approach. We consider people committed to our church when they are serving, giving, and involved in a small group, and accountability and discipleship happens within those groups. If we are the kind of church we need to be, we believe people will come. We don't have to pressure them or guilt them into coming. In fact, I (Corey) don't know who gives in the church financially and who doesn't. We keep a record of who comes, but we do not do an official membership process. One of the benefits we see in that approach is that if someone wants to leave because it is not a good fit, they don't have to get our "approval." Of course, I appreciate it when people do tell me, but they don't have to. They can leave and not feel guilty.

What about discipleship?

The discipleship process is a much bigger deal. It is the hardest process in our church as it is in any church. Clarity is a big deal with us regarding that. Our process is very simple and very basic. We move people through our vision statement which is Authentic Worship, Authentic Community, and Authentic Community Service. We view discipleship as a life-long process, not just a semester or a class or a program you necessarily go through. It's: "Are you plugged into the church?" "Are you plugged into a smaller group?" "Are you plugged into serving in some way?" And from that you may be called into full-time ministry in some way or into volunteer ministry. But discipleship is a big deal at our church and our goal is putting people into a process, not just having an event.

What are your majors and minors?

We believe in majors and minors. Things that we consider minors are things that we do talk about and address when they come up within the context of Scripture, but we don't feel they necessarily affect salvation. They are not "make or break" things for us. A couple of our "minors" are eschatology, Calvinism vs. Arminianism, differences in worship/church practices, Bible translations, and eternal security vs. conditional security.

We recognize that certain churches/denominations hold very strong beliefs on these issues, however we ultimately have found that these are things that don't affect our salvation. We have people in our church that differ in their beliefs over these issues and that's fine. Those issues speak from the

Scriptures to different people in different ways. For us, the issue of Jesus' death on the cross and His resurrection, the gifts of the Spirit, the fruit of the Spirit, and the infallibility of the Bible are major issues that we take pretty seriously.

What is your stance on debt?

We are a debt-free church. Since we have started, we have never had a credit card or taken out a loan. We only spend money that we have. We don't own the building we worship in; we rent it (although we have talked with elders and our landlord about the possibility of someday purchasing the building). We take this stance because the Bible says that the borrower is slave to the lender and because if we live within our means, we can do more within the community if we aren't millions of dollars in debt. We've actually had accountants and other financial people encourage us to take out loans and restructure our finances for various reasons and we feel very strongly that we shouldn't.

What is your belief about the gifts of the Sprit and their use in services?

Our Sunday services, we think, are for the everyman. That may mean for people who have never been to church, to the homeless, to millionaires, to people who have grown up in church. We cater to everyone on Sunday. We have very exuberant services, but they are very controlled. Everything is done within a time frame. They are not short—about an hour and a half or so. We are time conscious, but don't quench the Spirit. We want to make sure that if people are speaking in tongues loudly and exercising gifts, that it is under control and not being abused or used inappropriately. We teach the gifts of the Spirit, but we also teach that God is a God of order, not confusion. It is a fine line to walk when you have a church that is big where you teach and encourage the use of the spiritual gifts. There is always the chance for someone to get nutty and that's a hard balance to find sometimes.

How do you structure your services?

Our structure of service stays pretty consistent. We have a video ministry where we make our own videos. We open with a 5-minute pre-roll that uses artistic shots of town and people in the community along with people in the church. We go into a very energetic song. We do a community service video which is kind of a 30 second PSA of what we're doing in the community that month. That is followed by announcements and then three worship songs. Then I deliver the lesson using a PowerPoint presentation. We end with another song and then take communion. Communion is taken after every service.

Why do you take communion every service?

Communion is also a big deal to us. We don't think it saves your soul or that you have to take it, but it brings every service back to what Jesus did on the cross. So no matter what the lesson—whether it's Song of Solomon, or a vision service, or whatever--it all comes back to Jesus. We started doing communion this way, not because any of us came from a background where we did communion every week, but because I wanted to get everyone moving around and feeling comfortable and at home. So we started doing it this way and people liked it. It's also nice to see people do it with their family and friends and in small groups.

How do you get volunteers?

Our church has been put in a unique position because we have grown very rapidly. We don't have the luxury of being able to observe people for years because our church is so young. So we had to set in place some basic guidelines. If anyone wants to be involved in any area of volunteering in any capacity, they have to have attended for 60 days. We watch them to try to make sure they are stable and a good fit for us and also want to make sure that they believe the church is a good fit for them. Leadership is a different matter. We talk among the elders and staff and have to come up to some kind of unanimity that this is a good choice for this role.

What about baptism?

We have kind of an unorthodox approach to baptism. In our church we teach that anyone can baptize anyone else as long as they are a Christian. Therefore, we let mothers and fathers baptize their children as well as friends baptize friends. We let middle and high school students baptize. I have only done about a quarter of all the baptisms done at church. We believe that if you have led someone to the Lord then you can and should baptize them. It's just neat and makes it much more personal. It makes the idea of evangelism more tangible.

What is your hiring process?

With regard to hiring someone we go through a much longer process. We have an interview four or five times. They go through the executive pastor, the elders, and then one more meeting. Then I will take them and their spouse out to dinner and ask if they are in agreement and if the salary is enough for them to live on. I ask if their marriage and family can withstand the pressures of ministry.

Do you have any denominational affiliation?

No, our church is not a part of or affiliated with any denomination or church-planting networks. We have never taken any money from any denominations or outside groups. We left a denomination with a bad taste in our mouths because it was legalistic and controlling. Not all denominations are bad, but they can become a problem. Often we have felt there was a push to promote a "brand" or denomination rather than Christ. There are pros and cons. We have complete freedom to do what we feel is right, but you don't have the resources that come with denominational affiliation. There aren't camps and leadership retreats already in place to take advantage of so it takes a bit more work on our part because we don't have those connections. We at the Experience, therefore, take a little bit of pride in knowing that every chair we have bought and every person we have fed has come as a result of our own resources. What we have accomplished over the past five years has not come through connections, but from God. He sent us people with like minds and with like visions. And He gets all the glory!

Do you require seminary training?

Right now, no one that works at the church has had formal seminary education. It's not that we are opposed to it, but we have found in our church "secular" education and working out in the corporate world for a time has proved invaluable in our church culture. We have staff that have PhDs, Masters, and Bachelor's degrees, and some that haven't even been to college. We are not looking for a paper that says you are trained for ministry, we are looking for willing and teachable servants called by God to work in the mission field that is our city.

How do you study?

Since I do not have a degree from a seminary, though I do have a degree in English Literature, some wonder why or how I have the authority to teach the Word of God. I will not go into the fact that anyone can teach the gospel through the power of the Holy Spirit, but I will say that study and much time dedicated to commentaries and the Word itself is exceptionally important. I typically use very conservative sources and some more progressive ones, trying to find a balance and often times teaching both sides. I believe we need to offer options on the "minors" of scripture. Things like predestination and eternal security are things Christians can differ on, but still agree on the soul saving act of the cross.

What didn't work?

Oh, where to start? The biggest thing that did not work is trying to do more than you can afford or staff. As a new church, you shouldn't try to take on too much responsibility too fast. In fact, there are many things that your church should never do, especially if others in your city are doing well and you can simply complement their work instead of reinventing the wheel. Learn to say "no" to more than you say "yes" to, and make sure your vision statement is there to keep things in focus as the church expands and competing visions come into play.

What does the future hold?

You know, I keep getting asked at Next classes what our 5-year goals are, and I never really answer that question. I do my best by offering them a 3 year idea of what I think may happen, but if you would have asked me 6 years ago what I thought the church would look like, I could have never guessed we could have come this far.

So, here is my best attempt to guess at our future. Just about two hours before typing this, Patrick and I started to scope out a possible location for our second church plant. I know many churches have been doing this, but it is more uncharted waters for us. We are looking at two rural areas about a half hour away from our building that no one really wants to plant churches in. There is a big Baptist and big Church of Christ church in each town, which is fine, but we want to be the ones to offer community to the fringe in those small towns. We often ask people from those areas, "Where do people struggling with same sex attraction go if they are seeking God?" or "Are interracial couples comfortable in those churches in these rural areas?" and we long to fill the void that may be there.

Authentic Pursuit: Building a Church from Nothing

So, we plan to grow our church in Murfreesboro to its max capacity in its current location, then cap it if possible. We will then plant other churches, with other pastors and teams in rural areas about 30 minutes from where we are. Financially it makes no sense to plant in dying cities and towns, but we expect God to make dry bones come alive. The aim is to advance the Kingdom of God, not our kingdoms, but His.

If by chance you read this book and want to contact us about anything we can help with or any questions about our processes, videos, lessons, or just to come by and see our building and meet our staff:

www.experiencecc.com

info@experiencecc.com

615.707.0384

Made in the USA
Las Vegas, NV
10 September 2022